Bible Promises to Live By for Women

BIBLE PROMISES TO LIVE BY

for Women

KATHERINE J. BUTLER

Tyndale House Publishers, Inc.
Carol Stream, Illinois

Visit Tyndale online at www.tyndale.com.

TYNDALE, Tyndale's quill logo, New Living Translation, NLT, the New Living Translation logo, and LeatherLike are registered trademarks of Tyndale House Publishers, Inc.

Bible Promises to Live By for Women

Designed by Ron Kaufmann

General editor and writer: Katherine J. Butler

Scripture quotations are taken from the Holy Bible, New Living Translation, copyright © 1996, 2004, 2015 by Tyndale House Foundation. Used by permission of Tyndale House Publishers, Inc., Carol Stream, Illinois 60188. All rights reserved.

For information about special discounts for bulk purchases, please contact Tyndale House Publishers at csresponse@tyndale.com, or call 1-800-323-9400.

ISBN 978-1-4964-1807-4

Printed in China

23 22 21 20 19 18 17
7   6   5   4   3   2   1

CONTENTS

INTRODUCTION

Promises hold great power. When kept, they put our hearts at ease and give us assurance for the future. When broken, they can shatter our trust and leave us feeling disheartened and hopeless. God knows the immense power a promise holds and has filled his Word with promises for his people. Some of God's promises provide us with strength, perseverance, and encouragement to guide us through everyday life. Others speak to the deep desires inside each of us as we long to know that our future holds joy, security, purpose, value, and companionship. And because God has declared that his Word will last forever, we can trust him to keep each and every promise.

This book includes more than five hundred promises that come directly from God's Word. Each verse is drawn from the easy-to-read-and-understand New Living Translation. Arranged alphabetically by topic, this book allows you to find the promises that address your needs. The topics chosen are most relevant to the issues, concerns, and desires women face today. As you read, remember that God's promises are not for his people in general; they are for you *personally*. What do you long to hear God promise for your future?

Maybe you are in a season of great joy and blessing. Or perhaps you are in a place of great anxiety, fear, worry, and stress. No matter what season you find yourself in, God has specific assurances he wants to communicate to you through the promises in his Word.

Before you begin reading, ask how your life would be different if you really believed all of God's promises for you. You would probably be a more confident, peaceful, courageous, and secure woman. The more we meditate and reflect on God's promises, the more we see real change in our lives. Therefore, try your best to resist skimming over these promises. Read each one slowly, and allow it to sink deep into your mind and heart. This practice will truly transform your relationship with God and others. May God bless you as you take in the promises of the One who loves you and has promised wonderful things for your future.

ABANDONMENT

As women, one of our greatest fears is the termination of a cherished relationship and the loss and abandonment we feel from it. Whether abandonment comes through rejection, death, or divorce, we fear being left alone. One of the hardest consequences we face is the threat to our self-worth. How comforting it is, then, to know that God will never abandon us. We can be assured of this because he promises it time and again in his Word. Take heart that the one who loves you the most will never abandon you.

JOHN 6:37 | Those the Father has given me will come to me, and I will never reject them.

PSALM 94:14 | The LORD will not reject his people; he will not abandon his special possession.

PSALM 27:10 | Even if my father and mother abandon me, the LORD will hold me close.

2 CORINTHIANS 4:8-9 | We are perplexed, but not driven to despair. We are hunted down, but never abandoned by God.

JOHN 14:16 | I will ask the Father, and he will give you another Advocate, who will never leave you.

PSALM 9:10 | Those who know your name trust in you, for you, O LORD, do not abandon those who search for you.

PSALM 37:28 | The LORD loves justice, and he will never abandon the godly. He will keep them safe forever.

ABILITIES

We all go through times when we are tempted to believe that we have nothing new to offer the world. No matter how you are feeling, God says in his Word that none of his children are average—you have unique and special abilities to contribute to the Kingdom of God. Because of his grace, he has promised to give each of us gifts for doing certain tasks well. These gifts are not meant for us to boast about but rather are to be used for the good of the church and God's Kingdom. If you don't know your unique God-given abilities or how best to use them, begin by reflecting on the promises below. Trust that God has given you these gifts for a reason, and he will be faithful in showing you how to use them.

1 CORINTHIANS 12:7 | A spiritual
gift is given to each of us.

EPHESIANS 4:11-13 | Now these . . . gifts Christ gave to the church . . . to equip God's people to do his work and build up the church, the body of Christ . . . until we all come to such unity in our faith and knowledge of God's Son that we will be mature in the Lord, measuring up to the full and complete standard of Christ.

1 CORINTHIANS 12:18, 22-23, 26-27 | Our bodies have many parts, and God has put each part just where he wants it. . . . Some parts of the body that seem weakest and least important are actually the most necessary. And the parts we regard as less honorable are those we clothe with the greatest care. . . . If one part suffers, all the parts suffer with it, and if one part is honored, all the parts are glad. All of you together are Christ's body, and each of you is a part of it.

ZECHARIAH 4:6 | It is not by force nor by strength, but by my Spirit, says the LORD of Heaven's Armies.

PSALM 60:12 | With God's help
we will do mighty things.

*God has given us
different gifts
for doing certain
things well.*

ROMANS 12:6

AFFIRMATION

Most women have a deep need to feel affirmed —to know that our lives have meaning and that we are valued by others. When our husbands, children, friends, or coworkers don't offer the affirmation we need, we are left feeling rejected, alone, and worthless. However, God promises in his Word that he desires us more than anything. Your life matters greatly to him. It is impossible for God to forget you; he has promised that your name is written on his hand. When no one else offers you words of affirmation, be reassured that the almighty God loves you and desires a relationship with you—and not because of what you do but simply because of who you are.

GENESIS 1:27 | So God created human beings
in his own image. In the image of God he created
them; male and female he created them.

1 CORINTHIANS 15:3 | I passed on to you what was
most important and what had also been passed on to
me. Christ died for our sins, just as the Scriptures said.

JOHN 15:9 | I have loved you even as the
Father has loved me. Remain in my love.

1 THESSALONIANS 1:4 | We know, dear
brothers and sisters, that God loves you and
has chosen you to be his own people.

1 PETER 5:10 | In his kindness God called you
to share in his eternal glory by means of Christ
Jesus. So after you have suffered a little while,
he will restore, support, and strengthen you,
and he will place you on a firm foundation.

ISAIAH 49:15-16 | Can a mother forget her nursing child? Can she feel no love for the child she has borne? But even if that were possible, I would not forget you! See, I have written your name on the palms of my hands.

The mountains may move and the hills disappear, but even then my faithful love for you will remain.

ISAIAH 54:10

AGING

Our culture often associates aging with such physical traits as weight gain, wrinkles, and gray hair. But what if women of faith stood against the mainstream and decided to view aging differently? What if we saw it as an opportunity to reflect on God's care and faithfulness to us throughout the seasons of our lives? With this mind-set, we can be thankful and overjoyed for all of our years— a perspective that the young may not yet have. God promises many benefits to those who decide to live life with him by their side, so don't be discouraged by the passing of time and the changes in your body. Choose instead to reflect on God's promise to faithfully walk through every season of life with you.

> PSALM 71:6 | Yes, you have been with me from birth; from my mother's womb you have cared for me. No wonder I am always praising you!

> ISAIAH 46:4 | I will be your God throughout your lifetime—until your hair is white with age. I made you, and I will care for you.

> PROVERBS 3:1-2 | Store my commands in your heart. If you do this, . . . your life will be satisfying.

> PROVERBS 10:27 | Fear of the LORD lengthens one's life, but the years of the wicked are cut short.

> PSALM 92:12-14 | The godly will flourish like palm trees and grow strong like the cedars of Lebanon. For they are transplanted to the LORD's own house. They flourish in the courts of our God. Even in old age they will still produce fruit; they will remain vital and green.

ANGER

Of all our emotions, anger is one of the most difficult to control. Anger itself is not wrong; even God has righteous anger. But anger becomes a problem when it leads us to sin against God and others. God promises that our anger, when left unchecked, will have consequences. However, he also promises to be kind, merciful, and always ready to receive us with love. When you don't know how to control your anger, allow God's promises to give you perspective, encourage you toward godliness, and remind you of his endless grace.

PROVERBS 14:29 | People with understanding control their anger; a hot temper shows great foolishness.

PROVERBS 15:1 | A gentle answer deflects anger, but harsh words make tempers flare.

JAMES 1:20 | Human anger does not produce the righteousness God desires.

PROVERBS 11:29 | Those who bring trouble on their families inherit the wind.

PSALM 30:5 | His anger lasts only a moment, but his favor lasts a lifetime! Weeping may last through the night, but joy comes with the morning.

PSALM 103:8 | The LORD is compassionate and merciful, slow to get angry and filled with unfailing love.

PROVERBS 22:24-25 | Don't befriend angry people or associate with hot-tempered people, or you will learn to be like them and endanger your soul.

ROMANS 12:19 | Dear friends, never take revenge. Leave that to the righteous anger of God. For the Scriptures say, "I will take revenge; I will pay them back," says the LORD.

Sensible people control their temper; they earn respect by overlooking wrongs.

PROVERBS 19:11

ANXIETY

Anxiety stems from losing sight of God's goodness. It is a result of nesting on our fears and allowing the "what ifs" to plant doubt in our hearts. And as women, there are plenty of "what ifs" that cross our minds throughout the day. So what is the secret weapon to battling anxiety? When we choose to reflect on and trust in God's promises to care for us, anxiety loses its power. God tells us throughout his Word that he is good, that he loves us, and that he wants the very best for our lives. When we begin to accept that this almighty God is caring for us, we become women who are strong, secure, peaceful, and courageous.

1 PETER 5:7 | Give all your worries and
cares to God, for he cares about you.

PSALM 62:6 | He alone is my rock and my salvation,
my fortress where I will not be shaken.

JEREMIAH 29:11 | "I know the plans I have for
you," says the LORD. "They are plans for good and
not for disaster, to give you a future and a hope."

PHILIPPIANS 4:6-7 | Don't worry about anything;
instead, pray about everything. Tell God what you
need, and thank him for all he has done. Then you
will experience God's peace, which exceeds anything
we can understand. His peace will guard your
hearts and minds as you live in Christ Jesus.

BEAUTY

In many cultures, appearances are everything. Women who are physically attractive seem to get more attention, better breaks, and a taste of the good life. Because of this, it is tempting to believe that our outward beauty matters most. But does it really? God promises us that the condition of our heart is far more important than the appearance of our body. Even though most of us know this, we may have a difficult time truly believing it. However, the more we reflect on God's promises about the importance and benefits of inner beauty, the more we will be able to live in the reality of this truth. As you read through these promises, ask God to help you shift your focus from your physical appearance toward what will last for eternity.

PROVERBS 31:30 | Charm is deceptive, and beauty does not last; but a woman who fears the LORD will be greatly praised.

1 PETER 3:3-4 | Don't be concerned about the outward beauty of fancy hairstyles, expensive jewelry, or beautiful clothes. You should clothe yourselves instead with the beauty that comes from within, the unfading beauty of a gentle and quiet spirit, which is so precious to God.

1 SAMUEL 16:7 | People judge by outward appearance, but the LORD looks at the heart.

EZEKIEL 36:23 | I reveal my holiness through you.

1 CORINTHIANS 15:42 | Our earthly bodies are planted in the ground when we die, but they will be raised to live forever.

BELONGING

Have you ever felt like you didn't quite belong? Maybe you desire to feel more closely tied to a group of friends, better connected at church, or more comfortable within your own family. When you have faith in Jesus, he promises that you are completely and absolutely welcomed into his family, which includes all who have put their trust in him. The many benefits of being part of God's family include complete acceptance, a clear sense of purpose, victory over sin, an inheritance of real value, and the eternal security of knowing you will always belong. You can rest in the truth that no

matter where you are in life, nothing and no one
can take your place in his family.

PSALM 73:23-24 | Yet I still belong to you; you
hold my right hand. You guide me with your
counsel, leading me to a glorious destiny.

ISAIAH 26:19 | Those who die in the LORD will
live; their bodies will rise again! Those who sleep
in the earth will rise up and sing for joy!

LEVITICUS 26:12 | I will walk among you; I will
be your God, and you will be my people.

ISAIAH 43:1 | Listen to the LORD who
created you. . . . The one who formed you says,
"Do not be afraid, for I have ransomed you.
I have called you by name; you are mine."

GALATIANS 4:7 | Now you are no longer a
slave but God's own child. And since you are
his child, God has made you his heir.

PSALM 24:1 | The earth is the LORD's, and everything in it. The world and all its people belong to him.

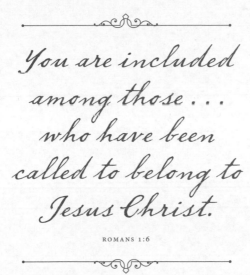

You are included among those . . . who have been called to belong to Jesus Christ.

ROMANS 1:6

BROKENNESS

Sometimes brokenness is the result of overwhelming circumstances. Other times it is a consequence of sin. No matter the cause, one thing is certain: Being in a state of brokenness allows you to realize that the only way out of your hurt and mess is by asking for God's help. This act signifies the breaking of your pride and self-sufficiency. You may feel your situation is too messy for God to handle, but remember that he is not afraid of it. God promises not only to be close to you in your brokenness but also that he will use it for your good. If you have been broken, come to God as a little child would, recognizing your neediness and utter dependence on him. Your brokenness has you in the perfect position for God to work his healing power in you. Take comfort in his promise to bind your wounds.

PSALM 34:18 | The LORD is close to the brokenhearted; he rescues those whose spirits are crushed.

PSALM 51:17 | The sacrifice you desire is a broken spirit. You will not reject a broken and repentant heart, O God.

PSALM 147:3 | He heals the brokenhearted and bandages their wounds.

MATTHEW 5:3 | God blesses those who are poor and realize their need for him, for the Kingdom of Heaven is theirs.

MATTHEW 18:4 | Anyone who becomes as humble as this little child is the greatest in the Kingdom of Heaven.

CHARACTER

We work hard all our lives to become excellent in many areas. We strive to excel in our work, marriage, mothering, friendships, ministries, and hobbies. Doesn't it make sense then to work just as hard at becoming morally excellent—to be known for character qualities like integrity, kindness, love, and faithfulness? The only way to grow in godly character is by spending time with our Lord. God promises we will become more and more like Jesus through the help of the Spirit as we continually seek a relationship with him and obey his Word.

GALATIANS 5:22-23 | The Holy Spirit
produces this kind of fruit in our lives: love,
joy, peace, patience, kindness, goodness,
faithfulness, gentleness, and self-control.

PHILIPPIANS 2:13 | God is working in you, giving you
the desire and the power to do what pleases him.

JOHN 15:5 | Yes, I am the vine; you are the branches.
Those who remain in me, and I in them, will produce
much fruit. For apart from me you can do nothing.

1 PETER 4:19 | Keep on doing what is right, and
trust your lives to the God who created you,
for he will never fail you.

MATTHEW 5:8 | God blesses those whose
hearts are pure, for they will see God.

COMFORT

Are you in a place or situation where you long to experience some comfort? Scripture promises us that God is faithful to provide us peace and rest when we need it. Sometimes we miss out on feeling his presence because we seek comfort in other ways. However, God is always near and promises to comfort us in a variety of ways. His comfort may come through his love, his Word, his presence, or his people. As you read through these promises, reflect on how God may be reaching out to you right now. Seek him in your times of need and watch him comfort you in ways you might never expect.

JAMES 4:8 | Come close to God, and
God will come close to you.

PSALM 138:3 | As soon as I pray, you answer me;
you encourage me by giving me strength.

PSALM 119:49-50 | Remember your promise
to me; it is my only hope. Your promise revives
me; it comforts me in all my troubles.

PSALM 119:52 | I meditate on your age-old
regulations; O LORD, they comfort me.

2 CORINTHIANS 1:3 | All praise to God, the
Father of our Lord Jesus Christ. God is our
merciful Father and the source of all comfort.

2 THESSALONIANS 2:16-17 | May our Lord Jesus
Christ himself and God our Father, who loved
us and by his grace gave us eternal comfort and
a wonderful hope, comfort you and strengthen
you in every good thing you do and say.

2 CORINTHIANS 1:4 | He comforts us in all our troubles so that we can comfort others. When they are troubled, we will be able to give them the same comfort God has given us.

Now let your unfailing love comfort me, just as you promised me, your servant.

PSALM 119:76

COMPARISON

The Internet and social media have made it almost impossible for us to keep from comparing ourselves to other women. When we feel like our homes, appearances, or possessions continually fall short, we must remind ourselves of God's promises in his Word. God assures us that when our thoughts are focused on him and his will, we will no longer feel the need to compare because the things of this world won't seem so important anymore. God promises a satisfying and fulfilling life when you look to him alone. Fix your thoughts on him, thank him for all you have now and all

you will receive for eternity, and watch how the
temptation to compare yourself to others begins
to disappear.

COLOSSIANS 3:2-4 | Think about the things of
heaven, not the things of earth. For you died to this
life, and your real life is hidden with Christ in God.
And when Christ, who is your life, is revealed to
the whole world, you will share in all his glory.

GALATIANS 6:4 | Pay careful attention to
your own work, for then you will get the
satisfaction of a job well done, and you won't
need to compare yourself to anyone else.

PHILIPPIANS 4:8-9 | And now, dear brothers and sisters,
one final thing. Fix your thoughts on what is true, and
honorable, and right, and pure, and lovely, and admirable.
Think about things that are excellent and worthy of
praise. Keep putting into practice all you learned and
received from me—everything you heard from me and
saw me doing. Then the God of peace will be with you.

This world is fading
away, along with
everything that
people crave.
But anyone who
does what pleases God
will live forever.

1 JOHN 2:17

CONFIDENCE

We all want to be women who exude confidence. Oftentimes we are most confident when we feel good about our clothes, our body, or the people we surround ourselves with. But these things only leave us feeling assured for a moment. Real and lasting confidence comes from knowing and trusting that God is on your side. What would it be like to live each day truly believing you are loved and cared for by the God of the universe? Most likely this belief would change the way you carry yourself. It would affect what you say and how you act. Reflect on God's promises about the benefits of loving him and belonging to him. They will give you confidence to live fully for him in this world because you'll know what awaits you for all eternity. Be confident in God's promises to watch over you, to give you what you need for each day, and to welcome you into his presence when you come face-to-face with him in heaven.

PSALM 118:8 | It is better to take refuge
in the LORD than to trust in people.

1 JOHN 4:4 | You belong to God, my dear children.
You have already won a victory over those people,
because the Spirit who lives in you is greater
than the spirit who lives in the world.

HEBREWS 6:18 | God has given both his promise
and his oath. These two things are unchangeable
because it is impossible for God to lie. Therefore,
we who have fled to him for refuge can have great
confidence as we hold to the hope that lies before us.

2 CORINTHIANS 3:11-12 | So if the old way, which has been replaced, was glorious, how much more glorious is the new, which remains forever! Since this new way gives us such confidence, we can be very bold.

EPHESIANS 3:12 | Because of Christ and our faith in him, we can now come boldly and confidently into God's presence.

Blessed are those who . . . have made the LORD their hope and confidence.

JEREMIAH 17:7

CONFLICT

Because we are sinful people, we are
bound to face conflict from time to time. Sometimes disagreements lead to greater understanding,
intimacy, and depth of relationship. Other times
they result in angry words, lingering bitterness, and
broken relationships. Therefore, how we choose to
respond to our conflicts is extremely important.
If you have a challenging relationship in your life
right now, take time to study God's Word and
reflect on his promises to bless those who work for
peace. It is never easy to be the person who takes
the high road, but God tells us that peacemakers

will experience his love, peace, and goodness in their lives.

2 CORINTHIANS 13:11 | Live in harmony and peace. Then the God of love and peace will be with you.

JAMES 3:18 | Those who are peacemakers will plant seeds of peace and reap a harvest of righteousness.

JEREMIAH 39:17-18 | I will rescue you from those you fear so much. Because you trusted me, I will give you your life as a reward. I will rescue you and keep you safe. I, the LORD, have spoken!

PSALM 118:7 | Yes, the LORD is for me; he will help me. I will look in triumph at those who hate me.

PSALM 34:14-15 | Turn away from evil and do good. Search for peace, and work to maintain it. The eyes of the LORD watch over those who do right; his ears are open to their cries for help.

MATTHEW 6:14 | If you forgive those who sin against you, your heavenly Father will forgive you.

God blesses those who work for peace, for they will be called the children of God.

MATTHEW 5:9

CONTENTMENT

Contentment is one of life's most elusive
qualities. We search for it in the money we make,
the possessions we accumulate, and the approval
we receive. The answer to "How much is enough?"
always seems to be "Just a little bit more." But true
contentment stems from being at peace with God,
which comes from accepting how he made you,
where he has placed you, what he has given you,
and who you are in relation to him. Contentment
is ultimately rooted in trusting God's power, pro-
visions, and promises. We grow in contentment
when we trust that God is in control, that he

knows what we need, and that he will work out his unique and wonderful plan for our life.

1 TIMOTHY 6:6-7 | True godliness with contentment is itself great wealth. After all, we brought nothing with us when we came into the world, and we can't take anything with us when we leave it.

HEBREWS 13:5 | Don't love money; be satisfied with what you have. For God has said, "I will never fail you. I will never abandon you."

PROVERBS 23:17-18 | Don't envy sinners, but always continue to fear the LORD. You will be rewarded for this; your hope will not be disappointed.

2 PETER 1:3 | By his divine power, God has given us everything we need for living a godly life. We have received all of this by coming to know him, the one who called us to himself by means of his marvelous glory and excellence.

I have learned how
to be content with
whatever I have.
. . . For I can do
everything through
Christ, who gives
me strength.

PHILIPPIANS 4:11, 13

COURAGE

Mark Twain once said, "Courage isn't
the absence of fear. It is acting in spite of it." Fear
is a natural part of life, and sometimes we have no
choice but to step into a situation that terrifies us.
However, we have the choice to move forward with
either timidity or courage. When you aren't feeling
very brave, trust that God is greater than any enemy
or problem you are facing. Throughout his Word,
God promises his people that he will give them
strength and courage and that he will never leave
them—and his words still hold true for you today.
Grow in courage by hoping in and trusting God's
promise to be with you wherever you go.

JOB 11:18 | Having hope will give you courage.

PSALM 27:1 | The LORD is my light and my salvation—so why should I be afraid? The LORD is my fortress, protecting me from danger, so why should I tremble?

DEUTERONOMY 31:6 | Be strong and courageous! Do not be afraid and do not panic before them. For the LORD your God will personally go ahead of you. He will neither fail you nor abandon you.

PSALM 18:31-33 | Who is God except the LORD? Who but our God is a solid rock? God arms me with strength, and he makes my way perfect. He makes me as surefooted as a deer, enabling me to stand on mountain heights.

PSALM 28:7 | The LORD is my strength and shield. I trust him with all my heart. He helps me, and my heart is filled with joy.

2 TIMOTHY 1:7 | God has not given us a spirit of fear and timidity, but of power, love, and self-discipline.

CRITICISM

It's easy to be overly critical—both of others and ourselves. There is a time and place for healthy, constructive criticism, but too often we criticize those around us simply because they are doing something that bothers us. However, our words are only helpful if they bring healing and encouragement to another. God has many promises about how to give and receive criticism in a way that honors him. Whether you are on the giving or receiving end, allow these promises to convict and encourage you toward speech that is gracious, truthful, loving, and a blessing to others.

EPHESIANS 4:29 | Let everything you say be good and helpful, so that your words will be an encouragement to those who hear them.

ROMANS 14:10 | Why do you condemn another believer? Why do you look down on another believer? Remember, we will all stand before the judgment seat of God.

JAMES 4:11 | Don't speak evil against each other, dear brothers and sisters. If you criticize and judge each other, then you are criticizing and judging God's law.

PROVERBS 12:18 | Some people make cutting remarks, but the words of the wise bring healing.

PROVERBS 15:31 | If you listen to constructive criticism, you will be at home among the wise.

1 PETER 4:14 | If you are insulted because you bear the name of Christ, you will be blessed, for the glorious Spirit of God rests upon you.

CULTURE

God's message has always been countercultural. If you are truly following Jesus and his teachings rather than the standards set by our culture, you will at some point be misunderstood, mocked, or possibly even persecuted. When you decide to stand against certain worldviews, act as Jesus would by praying for your enemies or giving away your money to those in need instead of spending it on yourself. These actions may not make any sense to the world around us. However, God promises many benefits to those who bravely choose to follow Jesus. Reflecting on his promises will give you strength, perspective, and encouragement to influence your culture instead of allowing your culture to influence you.

ROMANS 12:2 | Don't copy the behavior and customs of this world, but let God transform you into a new person by changing the way you think. Then you will learn to know God's will for you, which is good and pleasing and perfect.

PSALM 1:1 | Oh, the joys of those who do not follow the advice of the wicked, or stand around with sinners, or join in with mockers.

JOHN 8:12 | Jesus spoke to the people once more and said, "I am the light of the world. If you follow me, you won't have to walk in darkness, because you will have the light that leads to life."

ISAIAH 58:10 | Feed the hungry, and help those in trouble. Then your light will shine out from the darkness, and the darkness around you will be as bright as noon.

DEPRESSION

Sometimes what we most need during seasons of immense grief is to know we are not alone. If there is one thread of hope to hold on to in times of despair, it is that God is not afraid of our sadness. In fact, he promises to be with us in it. He listens to our prayers even when they feel empty, he gives us the support and strength we need to get through each day, and he sends his Spirit to pray for us when we cannot find the words. If you are in a place where it feels like you are sinking, be encouraged that there is no depth to which you can descend that he is not present with you. He is waiting there to comfort you and give you the strength you need to face another day.

PSALM 102:17 | He will listen to the prayers of the destitute. He will not reject their pleas.

2 SAMUEL 22:7 | In my distress I cried out to the LORD; yes, I cried to my God for help. He heard me from his sanctuary; my cry reached his ears.

ROMANS 8:26 | The Holy Spirit helps us in our weakness. For example, we don't know what God wants us to pray for. But the Holy Spirit prays for us with groanings that cannot be expressed in words.

2 SAMUEL 22:29 | O LORD, you are my lamp. The LORD lights up my darkness.

DEUTERONOMY 33:27 | The eternal God is your refuge, and his everlasting arms are under you.

PSALM 9:9 | The LORD is a shelter for the oppressed, a refuge in times of trouble.

He lifted me out of
the pit of despair.
. . . He set my feet
on solid ground
and steadied me as
I walked along.

PSALM 40:1-2

DESIRES

As women, sometimes our desires can feel overwhelming and confusing. In these moments it can be hard to trust whether our desires are right or wrong. But ask yourself this: Do the longings of my heart lead me away from the Lord or toward him? God promises that as long as we ultimately strive to know him, trust him, and seek his will, he will guide the desires of our hearts. When our greatest wish is to be in close relationship with him, that desire will influence all other desires. We can breathe a sigh of relief, knowing God is in control—even over our desires—and that he will help us long for the things that please him.

PSALM 145:19-20 | He grants the desires of those who fear him; he hears their cries for help and rescues them. The LORD protects all those who love him, but he destroys the wicked.

PSALM 37:3-4 | Trust in the LORD and do good.... Take delight in the LORD, and he will give you your heart's desires.

EZEKIEL 36:26 | I will give you a new heart, and I will put a new spirit in you. I will take out your stony, stubborn heart and give you a tender, responsive heart.

1 JOHN 2:16-17 | The world offers only a craving for physical pleasure, a craving for everything we see, and pride in our achievements and possessions. These are not from the Father, but are from this world. And this world is fading away, along with everything that people crave. But anyone who does what pleases God will live forever.

DISCOURAGEMENT

Feelings of discouragement are never from God but from Satan. He uses this tactic to steal our joy and courage and make us doubt the God we serve. When we notice discouraging thoughts creeping into our minds, we need to remember God's promises to us. His Word proclaims he is always with us, he will never fail us, and he will give us the strength to get through each day. With these promises in mind, what do we really have to be discouraged about? No matter what disappointments linger from our past or what impossible tasks hover over our future, remember that the God we serve is our greatest supporter and encourager.

1 CHRONICLES 28:20 | Be strong and courageous, and do the work. Don't be afraid or discouraged, for the LORD God, my God, is with you. He will not fail you or forsake you.

2 CORINTHIANS 7:6 | God, who encourages those who are discouraged, encouraged us by the arrival of Titus.

PSALM 42:5-6 | Why am I discouraged? Why is my heart so sad? I will put my hope in God! I will praise him again—my Savior and my God! Now I am deeply discouraged, but I will remember you.

JOSHUA 10:25 | Don't ever be afraid or discouraged. . . . Be strong and courageous, for the LORD is going to do this.

NEHEMIAH 8:10 | Don't be dejected and sad,
for the joy of the Lᴏʀᴅ is your strength!

Let's not get tired of
doing what is good.
. . . We will reap a
harvest of blessing
if we don't give up.

GALATIANS 6:9

ENDURANCE

Endurance isn't just about finishing well; it's about running the race well too. We all have moments when we feel tempted to cut corners, lose perspective, or just give up altogether, but with that attitude we don't make it very far. Endurance is about choosing to live each day well and striving to complete the tasks God has given us. With that mind-set, we can accomplish much. If you have the gift of serving others, serve them as if you were serving Christ. If you are a mother, love your kids better today than you did yesterday. If God has given you a specific assignment, complete it with excellence for his glory. Allow his promises to motivate you to keep going as they remind you that you are working toward something great. Remember that those who are faithful to the end will receive a greater reward than they could ever imagine.

HEBREWS 10:36 | Patient endurance is what you need now, so that you will continue to do God's will. Then you will receive all that he has promised.

HEBREWS 3:14 | If we are faithful to the end, trusting God just as firmly as when we first believed, we will share in all that belongs to Christ.

JAMES 1:2-4 | Dear brothers and sisters, when troubles of any kind come your way, consider it an opportunity for great joy. For you know that when your faith is tested, your endurance has a chance to grow. So let it grow, for when your endurance is fully developed, you will be perfect and complete, needing nothing.

ROMANS 2:7 | He will give eternal life to those who keep on doing good, seeking after the glory and honor and immortality that God offers.

ROMANS 5:3-4 | We can rejoice, too, when we run into problems and trials, for we know that they help us develop endurance. And endurance develops strength of character, and character strengthens our confident hope of salvation.

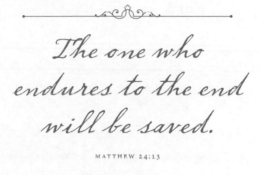

The one who endures to the end will be saved.

MATTHEW 24:13

FAILURE

Why is it that we are often so hard on ourselves? God doesn't beat us up for our mistakes and shortcomings, so why do we? The truth is that our God is a huge fan of second chances, third chances, fourth chances . . . and so on. Every day begins with fresh mercy and grace. No matter what circumstances have caused you to feel like a failure, bring them before God and ask for his guidance. He promises that he is faithful to forgive us and use our weaknesses for his glory. Visualize God right beside you, offering you his hand to help you get back onto your feet. Receive his help, and watch how his power shines best through your weakness.

JUDE 1:24-25 | All glory to God, who is able to keep you from falling away and will bring you with great joy into his glorious presence without a single fault.

LAMENTATIONS 3:22-23 | The faithful love of the LORD never ends! His mercies never cease. Great is his faithfulness; his mercies begin afresh each morning.

1 JOHN 1:9 | If we confess our sins to him, he is faithful and just to forgive us our sins and to cleanse us from all wickedness.

PSALM 37:23-24 | The LORD directs the steps of the godly. He delights in every detail of their lives. Though they stumble, they will never fall, for the LORD holds them by the hand.

2 CORINTHIANS 12:9 | Each time he said, "My grace is all you need. My power works best in weakness." So now I am glad to boast about my weaknesses, so that the power of Christ can work through me.

He has removed our sins as far from us as the east is from the west.

PSALM 103:12

FAITHFULNESS

One of the most challenging tests
the Lord may give in life is to trust in his faithfulness during difficult times. We fail at these tests
when we lose sight of God's big picture and trust
in things other than him. Therefore it is important
to continually strengthen our faith by reflecting
on his faithfulness toward us. God says he will
never fail us, forsake us, or break his promises to
us. If your trials are tempting you to lose heart
and doubt his faithfulness, think back to each time
when God has carried through on his promises to

you. Ask him to help you remember that you serve a God who can always be trusted.

DEUTERONOMY 7:9 | Understand, therefore, that the LORD your God is indeed God. He is the faithful God who keeps his covenant for a thousand generations and lavishes his unfailing love on those who love him and obey his commands.

PSALM 36:5 | Your unfailing love, O LORD, is as vast as the heavens; your faithfulness reaches beyond the clouds.

PSALM 103:17-18 | The love of the LORD remains forever with those who fear him. His salvation extends to the children's children of those who are faithful to his covenant, of those who obey his commandments!

DEUTERONOMY 32:4 | He is the Rock; his deeds are perfect. Everything he does is just and fair. He is a faithful God who does no wrong; how just and upright he is!

2 THESSALONIANS 3:3 | The Lord is faithful; he will strengthen you and guard you from the evil one.

PSALM 119:89-90 | Your eternal word, O LORD, stands firm in heaven. Your faithfulness extends to every generation, as enduring as the earth you created.

2 TIMOTHY 2:13 | If we are unfaithful, he remains faithful, for he cannot deny who he is.

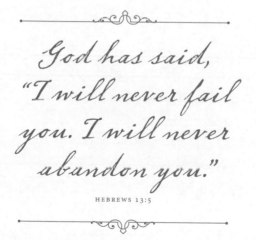

God has said,
"I will never fail
you. I will never
abandon you."

HEBREWS 13:5

FAMILY

Since God created families, you can be
reassured that he cares deeply about your family
and wants it to be a source of blessing, happiness,
and encouragement. Sadly, we live in a world where
many families do not get along this way. However,
God promises to bless those who recognize him
as the leader of their family and invite him into
their home. Whether you are a mother, stepmother,
grandmother, godmother, aunt, or sister, chances
are there are people who look up to you in your
family. Don't grow weary as you strive to be the
example of godliness, integrity, and faithfulness for

your family. Remember that the Lord promises not only to bless you but to bless entire generations who will follow your example.

PROVERBS 3:33 | The LORD . . . blesses
the home of the upright.

PROVERBS 14:11 | The house of the wicked will be destroyed, but the tent of the godly will flourish.

PSALM 112:1-3 | Praise the LORD! How joyful are those who fear the LORD and delight in obeying his commands. Their children will be successful everywhere; an entire generation of godly people will be blessed . . . and their good deeds will last forever.

PROVERBS 20:7 | The godly walk with integrity; blessed are their children who follow them.

ISAIAH 59:21 | My Spirit will not leave them, and neither will these words I have given you. They will be on your lips and on the lips of your children and your children's children forever. I, the LORD, have spoken!

FEAR

God must have known that the human heart would be prone to fear because we see it mentioned time and again throughout his Word. Interestingly, whenever God tells his people not to be afraid, he always reminds them of his presence with them. What are the things you fear today? God promises to be with you in the midst of them, so do you need to be afraid? No! The more we as believers reflect on God's presence, the less power fear has over our lives. That thing you fear the most might be the very thing that produces great faith in you. Remind yourself that your great and awesome God

is close beside you and will give you the strength
to stand strong in the face of fear.

PSALM 23:4 | Even when I walk through the darkest
valley, I will not be afraid, for you are close beside me.
Your rod and your staff protect and comfort me.

DEUTERONOMY 7:21 | Do not be afraid . . .
for the LORD your God is among you, and
he is a great and awesome God.

PSALM 46:1-2 | God is our refuge and strength,
always ready to help in times of trouble. So
we will not fear when earthquakes come
and the mountains crumble into the sea.

PSALM 91:5-6, 11 | Do not be afraid of
the terrors of the night, nor the arrow that
flies in the day. Do not dread the disease
that stalks in darkness, nor the disaster that
strikes at midday. . . . For he will order his
angels to protect you wherever you go.

ISAIAH 41:10 | Don't be afraid, for I am with you. Don't be discouraged, for I am your God. I will strengthen you and help you. I will hold you up with my victorious right hand.

I am leaving you with a gift—peace of mind and heart. . . . So don't be troubled or afraid.

JOHN 14:27

FINDING GOD

Many believers go through seasons where God's activity and presence in their lives seem absent. But we can be comforted by the truth that God never abandons those who seek him. If you begin each day by wholeheartedly searching for God, you will find him. How might God be working in your life at this very moment? Where was he present with you today that perhaps you failed to recognize? What events or people did he put in your day to remind you of his love? If you are in a season when God feels far away, remind yourself of his faithfulness and that he promises to reward those whose hearts sincerely seek after him.

2 CHRONICLES 15:2 | The LORD will stay with you as long as you stay with him! Whenever you seek him, you will find him. But if you abandon him, he will abandon you.

PROVERBS 8:17 | I love all who love me. Those who search will surely find me.

JEREMIAH 29:13-14 | "If you look for me wholeheartedly, you will find me. I will be found by you," says the LORD.

LAMENTATIONS 3:25 | The LORD is good to those who depend on him, to those who search for him.

HOSEA 10:12 | Plant the good seeds of righteousness, and you will harvest a crop of love. Plow up the hard ground of your hearts, for now is the time to seek the LORD, that he may come and shower righteousness upon you.

ACTS 17:27 | His purpose was for the nations to seek after God and perhaps feel their way toward him and find him—though he is not far from any one of us.

HEBREWS 11:6 | It is impossible to please God without faith. Anyone who wants to come to him must believe that God exists and that he rewards those who sincerely seek him.

MATTHEW 7:7 | Keep on asking, and you will receive what you ask for. Keep on seeking, and you will find. Keep on knocking, and the door will be opened to you.

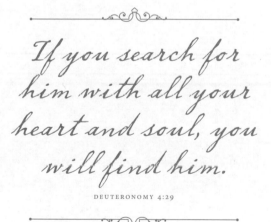

If you search for him with all your heart and soul, you will find him.

DEUTERONOMY 4:29

GOSSIP

Our words hold great power—even those we say behind another's back. Gossip is tempting because it makes us feel like we are in on a secret, but it is much more dangerous than we realize. God's Word tells us that gossip has the power to separate best friends, take away our good days, and lead us to sin. Likewise, when we learn to control our tongue and speak words of life to others, God promises it will reduce quarrels, help us avoid trouble, and lead to a happier life. Reflect on God's promises regarding the tongue while asking yourself if your words are kind, loving, true, and necessary.

MATTHEW 7:1 | Do not judge others,
and you will not be judged.

1 PETER 3:10 | The Scriptures say, "If you want to
enjoy life and see many happy days, keep your tongue
from speaking evil and your lips from telling lies."

PROVERBS 26:20 | Fire goes out without wood,
and quarrels disappear when gossip stops.

PROVERBS 16:28 | A troublemaker plants seeds
of strife; gossip separates the best of friends.

PROVERBS 10:11 | The words of the
godly are a life-giving fountain.

PROVERBS 12:13 | The wicked are trapped by their
own words, but the godly escape such trouble.

LUKE 6:45 | A good person produces good things
from the treasury of a good heart, and an evil person
produces evil things from the treasury of an evil heart.
What you say flows from what is in your heart.

GUIDANCE

As we get older, we face many tough decisions. From which college to attend and what career path to take to whom we'll marry and how we'll raise our children, these decisions bring up tough questions. *How do I know which way God wants me to go? Does he have a perfect plan for my life? What happens if I make the wrong decision?* When we find ourselves asking these questions, it is important that we open God's Word for guidance. He promises he will guide us, counsel us, lead us to truth, and help us hear his voice. And he always has our best interests at heart. Isn't it a gift to know you have a loving God who hasn't left you to figure out life on your own? When you are at a crossroad and need God's direction, surrender your request to him in prayer. Remember that he will guide you faithfully just as he promises in his Word.

PSALM 32:8 | The LORD says, "I will guide you along the best pathway for your life. I will advise you and watch over you."

PSALM 73:24 | You guide me with your counsel, leading me to a glorious destiny.

PSALM 25:10 | The LORD leads with unfailing love and faithfulness all who keep his covenant and obey his demands.

PSALM 48:14 | That is what God is like. He is our God forever and ever, and he will guide us until we die.

PSALM 16:7 | I will bless the LORD who guides me; even at night my heart instructs me.

JOHN 16:13 | When the Spirit of truth
comes, he will guide you into all truth.

PROVERBS 2:1, 9 | My child, listen to what I say. . . .
Then you will understand what is right, just, and
fair, and you will find the right way to go.

The LORD directs the
steps of the godly.
He delights in every
detail of their lives.

PSALM 37:23

HAPPINESS

Many of us make happiness our primary goal. We believe that if we can just have the right spouse, the perfect children, that job promotion, or a nicer house, then we will truly be happy. But the truth is that happiness has nothing to do with having ideal relationships, circumstances, or possessions; instead, it has everything to do with our daily relationship with our Lord. God's Word promises happiness to those who listen to its practical instructions. Do you strive to be godly? Does your heart honor the Lord? Do you place your hope in God alone? Do you delight in reading and obeying his commands? If you can honestly answer yes to these questions, then the Lord promises happiness. Still, there are seasons in life where it feels like the bad outweighs the good. If you are in that season, wake up each day asking the Lord to help you walk in his ways and grow closer to him. Trust that he will bring you happiness and a future you never thought possible.

PSALM 119:35 | Make me walk along the path of your commands, for that is where my happiness is found.

PROVERBS 10:28 | The hopes of the godly result in happiness, but the expectations of the wicked come to nothing.

PSALM 146:5 | Joyful are those who have the God of Israel as their helper, whose hope is in the LORD their God.

PSALM 112:1 | How joyful are those who fear the LORD and delight in obeying his commands.

PSALM 119:2 | Joyful are those who obey his laws and search for him with all their hearts.

HEALING

We all face moments in which we long for
healing. Whether we have a physical or mental ill-
ness, are battling a spiritual affliction, or feel the
ache of a trauma from our past, pain resides in
every one of us. When God's healing doesn't happen right away, we can become disheartened and
doubt his goodness. But God's Word promises us
two things in the midst of our pain. (1) He is able
to heal us, and (2) he honors the persistent prayers
of his people. He who made your body, mind,
and heart can certainly repair and restore them. If
you are longing for healing, don't lose heart. Keep

praying with persistence and trust that God will give you the strength you need to get through this season. Read his promises, and be encouraged that someday all your pain will be taken away. You will be healed once and for all.

EXODUS 15:26 | I am the LORD who heals you.

PSALM 73:26 | My health may fail, and my spirit may grow weak, but God remains the strength of my heart; he is mine forever.

PSALM 103:3 | He forgives all my sins and heals all my diseases.

JEREMIAH 30:17 | "I will give you back your health and heal your wounds," says the LORD.

MALACHI 4:2 | For you who fear my name, the Sun of Righteousness will rise with healing in his wings. And you will go free, leaping with joy like calves let out to pasture.

MATTHEW 7:11 | If you sinful people know
how to give good gifts to your children,
how much more will your heavenly Father
give good gifts to those who ask him.

PHILIPPIANS 3:21 | He will take our weak mortal bodies
and change them into glorious bodies like his own.

*O LORD, if you heal
me, I will be truly
healed. . . . My praises
are for you alone!*

JEREMIAH 17:14

HEAVEN

As women, with the many responsibilities on our plates, we often suffer from shortsightedness. We focus on the tasks of today and the problems waiting for us tomorrow. But God wants us to expand our field of vision, and he urges us to live with eternity in mind. That is why he has filled his Word with promises about heaven. These promises help us view life differently. They give us strength to persevere through trials because we know that this present life is not our final destination. The next time you face a problem or walk through a painful situation, reflect on the following verses. The more focused you are on your future with Jesus, the less attached you become to your own desires and plans and to the temporary attractions of this world. If you trust Jesus as your Savior, God promises there is a beautiful future in store for you for all of eternity.

JOHN 14:2 | There is more than enough room in my Father's home. If this were not so, would I have told you that I am going to prepare a place for you?

2 CORINTHIANS 5:1 | When this earthly tent we live in is taken down (that is, when we die and leave this earthly body), we will have a house in heaven.

1 CORINTHIANS 15:20 | In fact, Christ has been raised from the dead. He is the first of a great harvest of all who have died.

2 PETER 3:13 | We are looking forward to the new heavens and new earth he has promised, a world filled with God's righteousness.

ISAIAH 65:17 | Look! I am creating new
heavens and a new earth, and no one will
even think about the old ones anymore.

REVELATION 22:5 | There will be no night there—no
need for lamps or sun—for the Lord God will shine
on them. And they will reign forever and ever.

*God has made
everything beautiful
for its own time.
He has planted
eternity in the
human heart.*

ECCLESIASTES 3:11

HELPLESSNESS

Have you ever felt powerless to control or change a situation? It can be difficult to accept the reality that some things cannot be fixed no matter how hard you try. But perhaps feeling helpless is exactly where God wants you to be—not because it brings him joy to see you weak, but because it is only through your weakness that you will experience deep dependence on him. God has a special place in his heart for those who feel helpless. From cover to cover, God's Word is filled with his promises to listen to, comfort, defend, and protect the helpless. If you are in a place where you feel utterly helpless, God's promises will give you hope in his strength, power, and love.

PSALM 10:17 | LORD, you know the hopes of the helpless. Surely you will hear their cries and comfort them.

HEBREWS 4:16 | Let us come boldly to the throne of our gracious God. There we will receive his mercy, and we will find grace to help us when we need it most.

HEBREWS 13:6 | We can say with confidence, "The LORD is my helper, so I will have no fear. What can mere people do to me?"

ISAIAH 50:7 | Because the Sovereign LORD helps me, I will not be disgraced.

PSALM 10:12, 14 | Arise, O LORD! Punish the wicked, O God! . . . You see the trouble and grief they cause. You take note of it and punish them. The helpless put their trust in you. You defend the orphans.

PSALM 54:4 | God is my helper.
The Lord keeps me alive!

PSALM 9:12 | He does not ignore the
cries of those who suffer.

When we were utterly helpless, Christ came at just the right time and died for us sinners.

ROMANS 5:6

HOLY SPIRIT

When Jesus ascended into heaven, he promised his disciples (and believers everywhere) that he was leaving them with a gift: the Holy Spirit as their advocate, helper, source of strength, defender, teacher, and constant companion. Unlike those who lived during Old Testament times, these followers of Christ now had the Holy Spirit indwelling them— and as believers in Christ today, we do too. To really understand the benefits and blessings of the Spirit, we need to read God's Word. Reflect on God's promises about the Holy Spirit who lives in you. Allow your heart to praise God for his gracious gift.

EPHESIANS 1:14 | The Spirit is God's guarantee that he will give us the inheritance he promised and that he has purchased us to be his own people. He did this so we would praise and glorify him.

ACTS 1:8 | You will receive power when the Holy Spirit comes upon you. And you will be my witnesses, telling people about me everywhere.

ROMANS 8:26 | The Holy Spirit helps us in our weakness.

LUKE 12:11-12 | When you are brought to trial in the synagogues and before rulers and authorities, don't worry about how to defend yourself or what to say, for the Holy Spirit will teach you at that time what needs to be said.

JOHN 14:16-17 | I will ask the Father, and he will give you another Advocate, who will never leave you. He is the Holy Spirit, who leads into all truth.

JOHN 14:26 | When the Father sends the Advocate as my representative—that is, the Holy Spirit—he will teach you everything and will remind you of everything I have told you.

· ───── ·❦· ───── ·

We have received God's Spirit . . . so we can know the wonderful things God has freely given us.

1 CORINTHIANS 2:12

· ───── ·❦· ───── ·

HONESTY

Honesty isn't just about refraining from lying. It is about living a truly authentic life. This means avoiding exaggeration, manipulation, spinning events, and stretching the truth. It also means keeping promises, speaking the truth in love, and striving to live with integrity. God assures us that when we live a life of complete honesty, we have a wonderful future ahead. However, he also promises negative consequences to those who lie and give false accounts. Take an honest look at your life as you reflect on these promises. Ask God to show you how your speech and actions can be filled with authenticity and integrity.

PSALM 24:3-5 | Who may climb the mountain of the LORD? Who may stand in his holy place? Only those whose hands and hearts are pure, who do not worship idols and never tell lies. They will receive the LORD's blessing and have a right relationship with God their savior.

PSALM 32:2 | Yes, what joy for those whose record the LORD has cleared of guilt, whose lives are lived in complete honesty!

PROVERBS 19:5 | A false witness will not go unpunished, nor will a liar escape.

REVELATION 21:8 | Cowards, unbelievers, the corrupt, murderers, the immoral, those who practice witchcraft, idol worshipers, and all liars—their fate is in the fiery lake of burning sulfur.

PROVERBS 12:19 | Truthful words stand the test of time, but lies are soon exposed.

Look at those who are honest and good, for a wonderful future awaits those who love peace.

PSALM 37:37

HOPE

In our doubts and moments of weakness, holding on to hope is incredibly powerful. Hope keeps us from wavering in our faith; it anchors our souls to God. Losing hope puts us in danger of losing our faith as we take our eyes off of the God we love. That is why it is so important to remind ourselves daily of the hope we have in Christ. We serve a God who has given us his oath that he is the source of our joy, comfort, and peace in all our days on earth and that we will share in his glory later. When doubts fill your mind about the God you serve, hold on to hope and cling to his promises. He can be trusted to keep every single one.

HEBREWS 10:23 | Let us hold tightly without wavering to the hope we affirm, for God can be trusted to keep his promise.

ROMANS 15:13 | I pray that God, the source of hope, will fill you completely with joy and peace because you trust in him. Then you will overflow with confident hope through the power of the Holy Spirit.

PSALM 94:19 | When doubts filled my mind, your comfort gave me renewed hope and cheer.

PSALM 71:5 | O Lord, you alone are my hope.

HEBREWS 6:18-19 | God has given both his promise and his oath. These two things are unchangeable because it is impossible for God to lie. Therefore, we who have fled to him for refuge can have great confidence as we hold to the hope that lies before us. This hope is a strong and trustworthy anchor for our souls.

COLOSSIANS 1:27 | This is the secret: Christ lives in you. This gives you assurance of sharing his glory.

Hope in the LORD;
for with the LORD
there is unfailing
love. His redemption
overflows.

PSALM 130:7

HOSPITALITY

Sadly, many people are lonely, broken, and untrusting. They're in desperate need of kindness and love. So what hinders us from making an effort to seek these people out and invite them into our lives? As women, we sometimes avoid hospitality because we feel like our home or cooking is inadequate. Others of us may find it too difficult to share time, space, and resources. But beautiful decorations and gourmet meals have very little to do with hospitality. Hospitality is becoming a safe person and cultivating a safe space for others to experience the welcoming presence of God. And God promises many blessings to those who are hospitable to others. As you read these promises, ask the Lord to help you set aside your own discomfort and insecurities in order to be a woman who gladly practices hospitality.

LUKE 14:12-13 | Then he turned to his host. "When you put on a luncheon or a banquet," he said, "don't invite your friends, brothers, relatives, and rich neighbors. For they will invite you back, and that will be your only reward. Instead, invite the poor, the crippled, the lame, and the blind."

HEBREWS 13:2 | Don't forget to show hospitality to strangers, for some who have done this have entertained angels without realizing it!

MATTHEW 25:35-36, 40 | "I was hungry, and you fed me. I was thirsty, and you gave me a drink. . . . I was sick, and you cared for me." . . . And the King will say, "I tell you the truth, when you did it to one of the least of these my brothers and sisters, you were doing it to me!"

3 JOHN 1:5 | You are being faithful to God when you care for the traveling teachers who pass through.

God will reward you for inviting those who could not repay you.

LUKE 14:14

HUMILITY

Writer and philosopher C. S. Lewis states in his book *Mere Christianity*, "True humility is not thinking less of yourself; it is thinking of yourself less." We often mistake low self-esteem for humility. But that is not accurate according to God. Humility begins with knowing who God is and who we are in comparison. It is the antithesis of pride. It is not about seeing ourselves as less, but rather, seeing God as so much more. He is in ultimate control of everything, including our future, and his plans for our lives are far better than our own. When we view God this way, he promises to bless, honor, refresh, exalt, lead, and rescue those whose hearts are humble. As you read these promises, ask the Lord to help you think about yourself less so that you may focus on him more.

ISAIAH 55:8-9 | "My thoughts are nothing like your thoughts," says the LORD. "And my ways are far beyond anything you could imagine. For just as the heavens are higher than the earth, so my ways are higher than your ways and my thoughts higher than your thoughts."

LUKE 14:8, 10 | When you are invited to a wedding feast, don't sit in the seat of honor.... Instead, take the lowest place at the foot of the table. Then when your host sees you, he will come and say, "Friend, we have a better place for you!" Then you will be honored in front of all the other guests.

ISAIAH 66:2 | I will bless those who have humble and contrite hearts, who tremble at my word.

MATTHEW 18:4 | Anyone who becomes as humble as this little child is the greatest in the Kingdom of Heaven.

PSALM 25:9 | He leads the humble in doing right, teaching them his way.

PSALM 18:27 | You rescue the humble, but you humiliate the proud.

ISAIAH 57:15 | I restore the crushed spirit of the humble.

MATTHEW 23:12 | Those who exalt themselves will be humbled, and those who humble themselves will be exalted.

PSALM 69:32 | The humble will see their God at work and be glad. Let all who seek God's help be encouraged.

HURRY

We live in a culture that praises a busy and hurried lifestyle. When our lives are full of constant activity, we believe we are somehow more fulfilled or important than when we slow down and find time for rest. The truth is, however, that God did not intend for us to race through the only life we have been given. In fact, he promises that our rushing about is useless because we never know what the next moment will bring. When we fill our calendars with countless responsibilities, we leave little time to cultivate our relationship with God. Without quiet, focused time with

God, everything suffers. Intentionally put a stop to hurrying by slowly reading the verses below. Take a deep breath, calm your thoughts, and allow yourself to trust in God's promises. He has everything under control.

JAMES 4:14 | How do you know what your life will be like tomorrow? Your life is like the morning fog—it's here a little while, then it's gone.

PSALM 39:6 | We are merely moving shadows, and all our busy rushing ends in nothing.

COLOSSIANS 1:17 | He existed before anything else, and he holds all creation together.

EPHESIANS 1:21-22 | He is far above any ruler or authority or power or leader or anything else— not only in this world but also in the world to come. God has put all things under the authority of Christ and has made him head over all things.

ACTS 17:24-25, 28 | He is the God who made
the world and everything in it.... He himself
gives life and breath to everything.... For
in him we live and move and exist.

*Teach us to realize
the brevity of life,
so that we may
grow in wisdom.*

PSALM 90:12

INADEQUACY

God promises that he loves you—not because of your abilities, strengths, or talents, but because he is your Father. When you put your faith in Jesus as your Savior, God sees you as holy, as if you've never sinned. How can you not have "overwhelming victory" today when this is how the God of the universe views you? He is your strength and is able to do more through you than you could ever imagine. On days when you just don't feel like you are enough, rest in God's promises that he loves you deeply and will keep loving you no matter what. You are a person of great worth, and a person of

great worth can do mighty things because the very
Spirit and power of God is within you.

ROMANS 8:35, 37 | Does it mean he no longer loves
us if we have trouble or calamity, or are persecuted, or
hungry, or destitute, or in danger, or threatened with
death? . . . No, despite all these things, overwhelming
victory is ours through Christ, who loved us.

EPHESIANS 3:20 | All glory to God, who is able, through
his mighty power at work within us, to accomplish
infinitely more than we might ask or think.

HABAKKUK 3:19 | The Sovereign LORD is
my strength! He makes me as surefooted as
a deer, able to tread upon the heights.

1 PETER 2:9 | You are a chosen people. You
are royal priests, a holy nation, God's very own
possession. As a result, you can show others
the goodness of God, for he called you out
of the darkness into his wonderful light.

2 CORINTHIANS 4:7 | We now have this
light shining in our hearts, but we ourselves
are like fragile clay jars containing this great
treasure. This makes it clear that our great
power is from God, not from ourselves.

---

*I can do everything
through Christ, who
gives me strength.*

PHILIPPIANS 4:13

INTEGRITY

Throughout our lives every one of us will come to a crossroad where we will be faced with the choice to go down the right or wrong path. This choice is especially difficult when no one is watching or nearby to hold us accountable. However, God promises he is always watching and will someday judge all people for the decisions they make. He also promises to bless those who try to live with honesty, integrity, and pure hearts. The next time you must make a difficult choice between right and wrong, cry out for God's help, asking him to help you live each moment with integrity.

PSALM 5:12 | You bless the godly, O LORD; you surround them with your shield of love.

EPHESIANS 5:8-9 | Once you were full of darkness, but now you have light from the Lord. So live as people of light! For this light within you produces only what is good and right and true.

ECCLESIASTES 12:14 | God will judge us for everything we do, including every secret thing, whether good or bad.

1 PETER 3:12 | The eyes of the LORD watch over those who do right, and his ears are open to their prayers.

PSALM 97:11 | Light shines on the godly, and joy on those whose hearts are right.

PSALM 84:11 | The LORD God is our sun and our shield. He gives us grace and glory. The LORD will withhold no good thing from those who do what is right.

JEALOUSY

Jealousy is a feeling almost all women are familiar with. We wish for another woman's house, marriage, fashion sense, income, and dress size. If we aren't careful, our jealous thoughts become more frequent and come more naturally. When this happens, we need to remember that jealousy embitters us and eventually leads to harmful actions. God's Word warns that jealousy, if left unchecked, has the power to steal our joy, cause us to miss God's blessings, divide our families, and destroy relationships. When you begin to wish you were someone else or feel anger about what someone else has that you don't, jealousy is preparing to consume you. The antidote is to ask God to remind you of the blessings he has already given you and the promise of heaven he gives to all of his children for eternity. It is never too late to change your attitude, which has the power to change your life.

JOB 5:2 | Surely resentment destroys the fool, and jealousy kills the simple.

PROVERBS 14:30 | A peaceful heart leads to a healthy body; jealousy is like cancer in the bones.

JAMES 3:16 | Wherever there is jealousy and selfish ambition, there you will find disorder and evil of every kind.

PSALM 37:1-2 | Don't worry about the wicked or envy those who do wrong. For like grass, they soon fade away. Like spring flowers, they soon wither.

JOY

Joy doesn't come from how much we have, but rather how much we enjoy God. Do you enjoy God's presence? Do you allow yourself to taste and experience his goodness? Are you aware that he is singing a happy song over you this very moment? These are all reasons to rejoice! Take time to reflect on God's promises to those who love him and notice his blessings in their lives. Allow yourself to freely praise and thank him with a joyful heart for all that he has done and is doing in your life.

PSALM 9:2 | I will be filled with joy because of you. I will sing praises to your name, O Most High.

PSALM 16:11 | You will show me the way of life, granting me the joy of your presence and the pleasures of living with you forever.

ZEPHANIAH 3:17 | For the LORD your God is living among you. He is a mighty savior. He will take delight in you with gladness. With his love, he will calm all your fears. He will rejoice over you with joyful songs.

PSALM 128:1-2 | How joyful are those who fear the LORD—all who follow his ways! You will enjoy the fruit of your labor. How joyful and prosperous you will be!

JOHN 15:10-11 | When you obey my commandments, you remain in my love. . . . I have told you these things so that you will be filled with my joy. Yes, your joy will overflow!

PSALM 34:8 | Taste and see that the LORD is good. Oh, the joys of those who take refuge in him!

PSALM 22:26 | The poor will eat and be satisfied. All who seek the LORD will praise him. Their hearts will rejoice with everlasting joy.

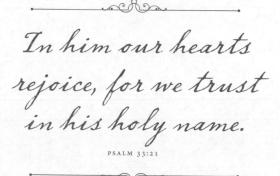

In him our hearts rejoice, for we trust in his holy name.

PSALM 33:21

JUSTICE

When we or someone we love has been hurt, something deep inside us cries out for justice. We want to make right the wrong that has been done, but we are not always able to do so. Thankfully, we have a God who cares deeply about injustice. He sees the ill-treatment and oppression of people. He has promised that those who do evil on this earth will not get away with it when he comes to judge the world. We do not have answers or solutions to all of life's tough issues, but we can trust that God does. The next time you ache for justice in this world, remember God's promises. Trust God to judge each situation perfectly because he is the perfect judge.

PSALM 96:12-13 | Let the trees of the forest sing for joy before the LORD, for he is coming! He is coming to judge the earth. He will judge the world with justice, and the nations with his truth.

2 THESSALONIANS 1:5-6 | God will use this persecution to show his justice.... In his justice he will pay back those who persecute you.

PROVERBS 20:22 | Don't say, "I will get even for this wrong." Wait for the LORD to handle the matter.

ROMANS 12:17-18 | Never pay back evil with more evil. Do things in such a way that everyone can see you are honorable. Do all that you can to live in peace with everyone.

ROMANS 12:19 | Dear friends, never take revenge. Leave that to the righteous anger of God. For the Scriptures say, "I will take revenge; I will pay them back," says the LORD.

PSALM 58:11 | Then at last everyone will say, "There truly is a reward for those who live for God; surely there is a God who judges justly here on earth."

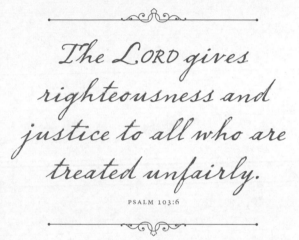

The LORD gives righteousness and justice to all who are treated unfairly.

PSALM 103:6

KINDNESS

Kindness is not weakness; nor is it flattery. Kindness is behaving toward others the way God behaves toward you. Sometimes it takes great effort to be kind to those we feel don't deserve it. But God's Word is filled with promises related to kindness. First, God promises always to be filled with kindness toward us and to bless us when we respond likewise toward others. When we strive to be kind, God promises our souls will be nourished and refreshed. We will gain a good reputation, and in the process, we will come to know God better. Allow God's kindness to motivate you to show kindness to others.

PROVERBS 3:3-4 | Never let loyalty and kindness leave you! . . . Then you will find favor with both God and people, and you will earn a good reputation.

PROVERBS 11:17 | Your kindness will reward you, but your cruelty will destroy you.

COLOSSIANS 1:9-10 | We ask God to give you complete knowledge of his will and to give you spiritual wisdom and understanding. Then the way you live will always honor and please the Lord, and your lives will produce every kind of good fruit. All the while, you will grow as you learn to know God better and better.

PSALM 145:8, 17 | The Lord is merciful and compassionate, slow to get angry and filled with unfailing love. . . . The Lord is righteous in everything he does; he is filled with kindness.

PSALM 116:5 | How kind the Lord is! How good he is! So merciful, this God of ours!

The generous will prosper; those who refresh others will themselves be refreshed.

PROVERBS 11:25

LISTENING

We often pray with the expectation that God will quickly solve all our problems. And when he doesn't, it is tempting to assume he isn't listening. Just because God isn't answering your prayers right now doesn't mean he isn't listening. Maybe one of the most loving things God can do for you in this season of waiting is to sit beside you and listen to your heart. We all have had times in our lives when it feels like our prayers just hit the ceiling. However, God tells us repeatedly in his Word that he always listens to us. If you are doubting whether God hears you, remind yourself of these promises. Trust

that he is loving you well by offering you his open
ears whenever you need to talk. Remember that
there are times when God's listening is far more
significant than anything else he could be doing
because through your conversations with him, you
are becoming the person he wants you to be.

PSALM 34:15 | The eyes of the LORD
watch over those who do right; his ears
are open to their cries for help.

ISAIAH 59:1 | Listen! The LORD's arm is not too weak
to save you, nor is his ear too deaf to hear you call.

1 JOHN 5:14-15 | We are confident that he hears us
whenever we ask for anything that pleases him. And
since we know he hears us when we make our requests,
we also know that he will give us what we ask for.

PSALM 55:17 | Morning, noon, and night I cry out
in my distress, and the LORD hears my voice.

PROVERBS 15:29 | The LORD is far from the wicked, but he hears the prayers of the righteous.

PSALM 116:2 | Because he bends down to listen, I will pray as long as I have breath!

The LORD hears his people when they call to him for help.

PSALM 34:17

LONELINESS

Loneliness is not an emotional or physical problem; it is a spiritual problem. We feel lonely because our sin has separated us from God. God created us for the very purpose of having a relationship with him. Therefore the pain of loneliness cannot be fixed by having more people in our lives. Our loneliness can only be cured when we accept Jesus as our Savior and trust his promises to always be with us. He desires to fill the holes in our hearts with his love and presence. If you are currently experiencing loneliness, view this season as an invitation to grow close to God. He has promised to

155

go before you and follow you through each step of
your journey.

ROMANS 8:38-39 | I am convinced that nothing can
ever separate us from God's love. Neither death nor life,
neither angels nor demons, neither our fears for today
nor our worries about tomorrow—not even the powers
of hell can separate us from God's love. No power in
the sky above or in the earth below—indeed, nothing
in all creation will ever be able to separate us from the
love of God that is revealed in Christ Jesus our Lord.

PSALM 16:8 | I know the LORD is always with me.
I will not be shaken, for he is right beside me.

JOHN 14:16 | [Jesus said,] "I will ask the Father, and he
will give you another Advocate, who will never leave you."

PSALM 139:5 | You go before me and follow me.
You place your hand of blessing on my head.

PSALM 145:18 | The LORD is close to all who call
on him, yes, to all who call on him in truth.

LOSS

The Bible states that sorrow and grief are part of human life, even for those who love God. Perhaps the most difficult part of loss is accepting the reality that someone or something you love is gone—and then beginning the process of letting go. Whether your loss was predictable and necessary or random and tragic, it will have a profound impact on you. But Scripture does not allow sorrow to have the last word. God promises to redeem our losses with comfort and hope. He promises to dry every tear from our eyes and give us a future where sorrow will be no more.

ISAIAH 25:8 | He will swallow up death forever!
The Sovereign LORD will wipe away all tears.

REVELATION 21:4 | He will wipe every tear from
their eyes, and there will be no more death or sorrow
or crying or pain. All these things are gone forever.

MATTHEW 5:4 | God blesses those who
mourn, for they will be comforted.

PSALM 56:8 | You keep track of all my sorrows.
You have collected all my tears in your bottle.
You have recorded each one in your book.

LAMENTATIONS 3:19-22 | The thought of my
suffering and homelessness is bitter beyond words.
I will never forget this awful time, as I grieve over
my loss. Yet I still dare to hope when I remember
this: The faithful love of the LORD never ends!

LAMENTATIONS 3:32 | Though he brings
grief, he also shows compassion because
of the greatness of his unfailing love.

LOVE OF GOD

Do you find it easy to believe that God loves the world but much harder to believe that God loves you as an individual? God's love for you began before you were born, and it continues throughout your life, extending through eternity. His promises of love ought to be the foundation for how you live, make decisions, and relate to others. If you approach each day with the confidence that you are loved by God, you can remain secure and joyful—even when circumstances stand against you. Reflect on these promises and ask God to help you internalize the truths of his special, unique love for you.

1 JOHN 4:9-10 | God showed how much he loved us by sending his one and only Son into the world so that we might have eternal life through him. This is real love—not that we loved God, but that he loved us and sent his Son as a sacrifice to take away our sins.

PSALM 23:6 | Surely your goodness and unfailing love will pursue me all the days of my life.

PSALM 31:7 | I will be glad and rejoice in your unfailing love, for you have seen my troubles, and you care about the anguish of my soul.

EPHESIANS 3:17-18 | Christ will make his home in your hearts as you trust in him. Your roots will grow down into God's love and keep you strong. And may you have the power to understand, as all God's people should, how wide, how long, how high, and how deep his love is.

DEUTERONOMY 5:10 | I lavish unfailing love for a thousand generations on those who love me and obey my commands.

1 JOHN 3:1 | See how very much our Father loves us, for he calls us his children, and that is what we are!

PSALM 145:8 | The LORD is merciful and compassionate, slow to get angry and filled with unfailing love.

God showed his great love for us by sending Christ to die for us while we were still sinners.

ROMANS 5:8

MARRIAGE

Marriage was God's idea from the beginning. He knew it wasn't good for men and women to be alone, so he designed marriage to bring us joy, intimacy, companionship, and blessing. But when two imperfect people come together, they are bound to have times of conflict and disappointment. For that reason, God has given us specific instructions for relationships. A wife who pleases the Lord is filled with love, honors her marriage by staying faithful, overlooks the small stuff, and does her best to exemplify Jesus to her spouse. Even so, some women have done all the right things and still find themselves in a lonely, unfulfilling marriage. God has special promises for the lonely in marriage too. No matter what your marriage looks like today, come to God's Word for wisdom and encouragement. Allow his promises to convict and encourage you to be a wife who loves and honors your husband and your God.

EPHESIANS 5:2 | Live a life filled with love, following the example of Christ. He loved us and offered himself as a sacrifice for us, a pleasing aroma to God.

COLOSSIANS 3:14 | Above all, clothe yourselves with love, which binds us all together in perfect harmony.

ISAIAH 54:5-6 | Your Creator will be your husband; the LORD of Heaven's Armies is his name! He is your Redeemer, the Holy One of Israel, the God of all the earth. For the LORD has called you back from your grief—as though you were a young wife abandoned by her husband.

PROVERBS 19:11 | Sensible people control their temper; they earn respect by overlooking wrongs.

PSALM 147:3 | He heals the brokenhearted and bandages their wounds.

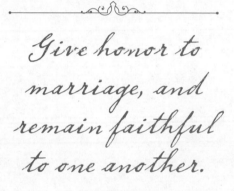

Give honor to marriage, and remain faithful to one another.

HEBREWS 13:4

MEDIOCRITY

Before you were born, God formed you in your mother's womb and chose you as his daughter. He knows you intimately and calls you a member of his family. No matter how ordinary and insignificant your life may seem, God has promised that you are special to him, and he made you for a purpose. Don't be tempted to believe that you are mediocre or that your life doesn't matter. Walk with confidence and start living like you are a child of the Most High God. Your Father doesn't just have something great in store for your future—he has something great in store for you *today*. Reflect on

167

these promises, and allow the truth to sink in that the almighty God will fulfill his purpose for you.

> JEREMIAH 1:5 | I knew you before I formed you in your mother's womb. Before you were born I set you apart and appointed you.

> JAMES 1:18 | He chose to give birth to us by giving us his true word. And we, out of all creation, became his prized possession.

> EPHESIANS 2:19 | You are members of God's family.

> JOHN 15:16 | You didn't choose me. I chose you. I appointed you to go and produce lasting fruit, so that the Father will give you whatever you ask for, using my name.

> ROMANS 12:4-5 | Just as our bodies have many parts and each part has a special function, so it is with Christ's body. We are many parts of one body, and we all belong to each other.

ROMANS 8:29 | God knew his people in advance,
and he chose them to become like his Son.

---

*I cry out to
God Most High,
to God who
will fulfill his
purpose for me.*

PSALM 57:2

MERCY

When others wrong us, we cry out for justice. When we wrong God, we cry out for mercy. Fortunately, God promises to be merciful to us. He shows his mercy through his compassion and not punishing us as we deserve. Have you felt the love and forgiveness of God at a time when you knew you didn't deserve it? How might his promises of mercy encourage you to be merciful to others today? If God's great mercy is hard to accept, reflect on what the Bible proclaims about God's great love. He shows mercy for one reason and one reason only—because he loves you so much.

2 SAMUEL 24:14 | Let us fall into the hands of the LORD, for his mercy is great.

PSALM 103:10 | [The Lord] does not punish us for all our sins; he does not deal harshly with us, as we deserve.

MATTHEW 5:7 | God blesses those who are merciful, for they will be shown mercy.

EXODUS 34:6 | The LORD passed in front of Moses, calling out, "Yahweh! The LORD! The God of compassion and mercy! I am slow to anger and filled with unfailing love and faithfulness."

EPHESIANS 2:4-5 | God is so rich in mercy, and he loved us so much, that even though we were dead because of our sins, he gave us life.

DANIEL 9:9 | The Lord our God is merciful and forgiving, even though we have rebelled against him.

MONEY

When it comes to money, the world encourages us to make more, spend more, and live with more. But God has a much different view. He doesn't focus on how much money we have, but rather on how generous we are with it. He promises that those who give freely and cheerfully will be generously rewarded in return. Who in your life might God be calling you to share your money with? Will his promises regarding money encourage you to give a little more than what you are comfortable with? Ask God to help you have his perspective on money so you can receive the joys and benefits promised to those who give generously.

PROVERBS 28:27 | Whoever gives to the poor will lack nothing, but those who close their eyes to poverty will be cursed.

2 CORINTHIANS 9:6 | Remember this—a farmer who plants only a few seeds will get a small crop. But the one who plants generously will get a generous crop.

LUKE 6:38 | Give, and you will receive. Your gift will return to you in full—pressed down, shaken together to make room for more, running over, and poured into your lap. The amount you give will determine the amount you get back.

2 CORINTHIANS 9:7-8 | You must each decide in your heart how much to give. And don't give reluctantly or in response to pressure. "For God loves a person who gives cheerfully." And God will generously provide all you need. Then you will always have everything you need and plenty left over to share with others.

1 TIMOTHY 6:17-19 | Teach those who are rich in this world not to be proud and not to trust in their money, which is so unreliable. Their trust should be in God, who richly gives us all we need for our enjoyment. Tell them to use their money to do good. They should be rich in good works and generous to those in need, always being ready to share with others. By doing this they will be storing up their treasure as a good foundation for the future so that they may experience true life.

The generous will prosper.

PROVERBS 11:25

NEEDS

Growing up, we're taught that neediness is a bad thing. Instead, we're praised when we're independent and self-sufficient. However, God teaches that when we realize our need for him, we are truly blessed. Being in need puts us in a position of humble dependence on him, and this kind of dependence requires us to trust that God truly knows what we need. Because of this truth, we can face tomorrow without worry. Remember that God doesn't promise to give us everything we want—he promises to give us everything we need. Take one day at a time, surrendering your needs to him. God promises that those who trust and fear him will lack nothing.

PHILIPPIANS 4:19 | This same God who takes care of me will supply all your needs from his glorious riches, which have been given to us in Christ Jesus.

PSALM 9:18 | The needy will not be ignored forever; the hopes of the poor will not always be crushed.

PSALM 34:9 | Fear the LORD, you his godly people, for those who fear him will have all they need.

MATTHEW 5:3 | God blesses those who are poor and realize their need for him, for the Kingdom of Heaven is theirs.

MATTHEW 6:33 | Seek the Kingdom of God above all else, and live righteously, and he will give you everything you need.

PSALM 22:24 | He has not ignored or belittled the suffering of the needy. He has not turned his back on them, but has listened to their cries for help.

PSALM 23:1 | The LORD is my shepherd; I have all that I need.

OVERWHELMED

Have you ever been so overwhelmed that it made you feel paralyzed and powerless? Maybe your burdens weighed on you so heavily that you felt you were sinking in a great ocean of hopelessness. It's overwhelming enough to deal with the stresses and problems of everyday life, but looking into the future and seeing all the obstacles ahead can send us over the edge. No matter what trouble, grief, or stressor you are facing today, God promises to be with you—guiding you, comforting you, and restoring your hope. Pour your heart out to him, and trust that he is able to lift you up above your circumstances and give your heart the strength it needs.

PSALM 145:14 | The LORD helps the fallen and lifts those bent beneath their loads.

PSALM 55:22 | Give your burdens to the LORD, and he will take care of you. He will not permit the godly to slip and fall.

PSALM 142:3 | When I am overwhelmed, you alone know the way I should turn.

PSALM 62:8 | O my people, trust in him at all times. Pour out your heart to him, for God is our refuge.

2 CORINTHIANS 1:8-9 | We were crushed and overwhelmed beyond our ability to endure, and we thought we would never live through it. In fact, we expected to die. But as a result, we stopped relying on ourselves and learned to rely only on God, who raises the dead.

PATIENCE

Patience is an active choice to gracefully wait for something to unfold. God promises that when we patiently face situations with perseverance and endurance, he will help us, honor us, give us hope and encouragement, and be pleased with us. What situation in life is currently testing your patience? How might God's promises encourage you to respond to this frustrating circumstance with grace and self-control? Whether you spent two hours stuck in rush-hour traffic today or held a crying baby at 2:00 a.m., God is using these moments to grow you into a patient woman. Ask him to help you continue on with patient endurance, and watch the fruit it will produce in your life.

JAMES 1:12 | God blesses those who patiently endure testing and temptation. Afterward they will receive the crown of life that God has promised to those who love him.

PSALM 40:1 | I waited patiently for the LORD to help me, and he turned to me and heard my cry.

ROMANS 15:4-5 | Such things were written in the Scriptures long ago to teach us. And the Scriptures give us hope and encouragement as we wait patiently for God's promises to be fulfilled. May God, who gives this patience and encouragement, help you live in complete harmony with each other, as is fitting for followers of Christ Jesus.

1 PETER 2:20 | Of course, you get no credit for being patient if you are beaten for doing wrong. But if you suffer for doing good and endure it patiently, God is pleased with you.

JAMES 5:7-8 | Dear brothers and sisters, be patient as you wait for the Lord's return. Consider the farmers who patiently wait for the rains in the fall and in the spring. They eagerly look for the valuable harvest to ripen. You, too, must be patient. Take courage, for the coming of the Lord is near.

Be still in the presence of the LORD, and wait patiently for him to act.

PSALM 37:7

PEACE

Do you long for peace in the midst of your unpredictable, messy, and chaotic life? No matter how frayed your nerves are or how unsettled your heart feels, God is able to calm you. Peace doesn't come naturally just because we are believers. God's Word advises us to actively pursue it. God promises peace to those who strive to know his Word, follow his commands, trust him at all times, live in harmony with others, and keep their thoughts focused on him. Which of these areas do you need to work on to experience his peace? Be encouraged that God longs to calm your heart and help you experience the kind of peace he has to offer.

PHILIPPIANS 4:9 | Keep putting into practice all you learned and received from me— everything you heard from me and saw me doing. Then the God of peace will be with you.

LEVITICUS 26:6 | I will give you peace . . . and you will be able to sleep with no cause for fear.

PSALM 119:165 | Those who love your instructions have great peace and do not stumble.

ISAIAH 48:18 | Oh, that you had listened to my commands! Then you would have had peace flowing like a gentle river and righteousness rolling over you like waves in the sea.

PSALM 4:8 | In peace I will lie down and sleep, for you alone, O LORD, will keep me safe.

ISAIAH 26:3 | You will keep in perfect peace all who trust in you, all whose thoughts are fixed on you!

2 CORINTHIANS 13:11 | Be joyful. Grow to maturity.
Encourage each other. Live in harmony and peace.
Then the God of love and peace will be with you.

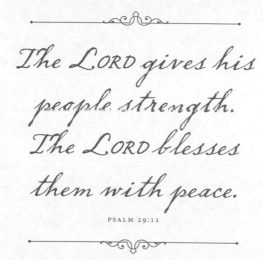

The LORD gives his people strength. The LORD blesses them with peace.

PSALM 29:11

PERFECTIONISM

Striving for perfection can be exhausting. We know it is an impossible standard, yet there is a part of us that believes we can reach it. The truth is, no matter how hard you try, you will never obtain the perfection you seek in this world. But God may be calling you to a different kind of "perfection." Though you cannot be made perfect through your own effort, you can be made holy and blameless before God because of his. God offered his Son as a sacrifice for your sins, and when you accept this gift and believe in Jesus Christ with your whole heart, God calls you holy, without fault, and free by his grace! Isn't that kind of perfectionism much better than the world's? Relinquish perfectionism and accept who you really are—an imperfect person who has been made perfect because of what God has done for you.

COLOSSIANS 1:22 | Now he has reconciled you to himself through the death of Christ in his physical body. As a result, he has brought you into his own presence, and you are holy and blameless as you stand before him without a single fault.

HEBREWS 10:14 | By that one offering he forever made perfect those who are being made holy.

GALATIANS 3:3, 7 | How foolish can you be? After starting your new lives in the Spirit, why are you now trying to become perfect by your own human effort? . . . The real children of Abraham, then, are those who put their faith in God.

ROMANS 6:14 | Sin is no longer your master, for
you no longer live under the requirements of the law.
Instead, you live under the freedom of God's grace.

*Even perfection
has its limits,
but your commands
have no limit.*

PSALM 119:96

PLANNING

Some of us love to plan. We like to know what lies ahead so we can be prepared for any circumstance. Planning is a wise and necessary part of life; however, some of us do so because it helps us to feel in control. Thankfully God is also a planner and a really good one at that. He promises he has a great plan for all who trust in him. What would it be like for you to release control to the God who is good, loving, powerful, and sovereign? After all, we are not guaranteed tomorrow and can benefit greatly from relinquishing control and trusting his plans for our lives. Relax in his promises that he

will ultimately work out his good and perfect will
for your life.

> PROVERBS 19:21 | You can make many plans,
> but the LORD's purpose will prevail.

> PSALM 138:8 | The LORD will work out his plans for my
> life—for your faithful love, O LORD, endures forever.

> PSALM 139:3 | You see me when I travel and
> when I rest at home. You know everything I do.

> ISAIAH 14:26-27 | I have a plan for the whole earth,
> a hand of judgment upon all the nations. The LORD
> of Heaven's Armies has spoken—who can change his
> plans? When his hand is raised, who can stop him?

> EPHESIANS 1:9-10 | God has now revealed to us his
> mysterious will regarding Christ—which is to fulfill his
> own good plan. And this is the plan: At the right time
> he will bring everything together under the authority
> of Christ—everything in heaven and on earth.

POWER OF GOD

God created the heavens and the earth and holds all of creation together. If God is this powerful, then surely he is able to do the impossible for you. Is there a situation in your life where you feel tempted to doubt God's power at work? Trusting in his power means you don't have to try so hard. You can relax knowing that your almighty Father is on your side. The next time the enemy tempts you to doubt or underestimate God's power, pray with boldness. Remind yourself that with God, anything is possible.

MARK 9:23 | "What do you mean, 'If I can'?" Jesus asked. "Anything is possible if a person believes."

JOHN 10:28-29 | I give them eternal life, and they will never perish. No one can snatch them away from me, for my Father has given them to me, and he is more powerful than anyone else. No one can snatch them from the Father's hand.

LUKE 18:27 | What is impossible for people is possible with God.

COLOSSIANS 1:16-17 | Through [Christ] God created everything in the heavenly realms and on earth. He made the things we can see and the things we can't see—such as thrones, kingdoms, rulers, and authorities in the unseen world. Everything was created through him and for him. He existed before anything else, and he holds all creation together.

MATTHEW 19:26 | With God everything is possible.

MARK 11:22-23 | Have faith in God. I tell you the truth, you can say to this mountain, "May you be lifted up and thrown into the sea," and it will happen. But you must really believe it will happen and have no doubt in your heart.

ISAIAH 45:18 | The LORD is God, and he created the heavens and earth and put everything in place. He made the world to be lived in, not to be a place of empty chaos. "I am the LORD," he says, "and there is no other."

Is anything too hard for the LORD?

GENESIS 18:14

PRAYER

Have you ever called out to God when you were in trouble? Pleaded with him over something important to you? Wept before him as you repented? God loves the sincere prayers of his people. And he promises to answer each and every one of them. Sometimes he graciously chooses to answer prayers with an astounding "Yes!" Other times, he answers them in ways we never expect. Yet we can be confident that God will *always* answer in his timing. Whatever you have been praying for, don't give up. God can be trusted with your prayers. He promises to faithfully answer the sincere prayers of those who trust in him.

JAMES 5:16 | The earnest prayer of a righteous person has great power and produces wonderful results.

PSALM 116:1 | I love the LORD because he hears my voice and my prayer for mercy.

PSALM 65:5 | You faithfully answer our prayers with awesome deeds, O God our savior.

PSALM 6:8-9 | Go away, all you who do evil, for the LORD has heard my weeping. The LORD has heard my plea; the LORD will answer my prayer.

PSALM 4:3 | You can be sure of this: The LORD set apart the godly for himself. The LORD will answer when I call to him.

PSALM 65:1-2 | What mighty praise, O God, belongs to you . . . for you answer our prayers.

PRESENCE OF GOD

The greatest gift we could ever receive is the loving presence of another. Whether you are aware of it or not, God is always with you, working on your behalf. And he desires closeness with you! Thoughts of worry, discouragement, fear, self-pity, distraction, and hopelessness lose their power over you as you grow in awareness of God's presence. What causes you to miss the presence and activity of God in your life? The next time you are tempted to believe you are alone in this world, remember that God is with you every moment of every day. Don't miss what he is doing right in front of you!

Read these promises and pray for God to open your eyes to his work and presence with you today.

MATTHEW 1:23 | Look! The virgin will conceive a child! She will give birth to a son, and they will call him Immanuel, which means "God is with us."

1 JOHN 4:9-10 | God showed how much he loved us by sending his one and only Son into the world so that we might have eternal life through him. This is real love—not that we loved God, but that he loved us and sent his Son as a sacrifice to take away our sins.

JOHN 1:14 | The Word became human and made his home among us. He was full of unfailing love and faithfulness. And we have seen his glory, the glory of the Father's one and only Son.

JEREMIAH 31:3 | Long ago the LORD said ... "I have loved you, my people, with an everlasting love. With unfailing love I have drawn you to myself."

REVELATION 21:3 | Look, God's home is now among his people! He will live with them, and they will be his people. God himself will be with them.

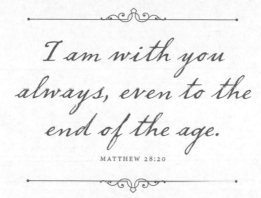

I am with you always, even to the end of the age.

MATTHEW 28:20

PROTECTION

How can we understand God's promises of protection in a world rife with sadness and tragedy? Perhaps God's view of protection is much larger and more significant than ours. While God cares for us and our physical safety, he is more concerned about our spiritual protection. When we view our earthly life and eternal future with this perspective, God's promises of protection take on a much deeper meaning. Bad things will continue to happen in our lifetime, but none so bad that they will separate us from him. Sad things will happen too, but nothing so sad that God cannot redeem them.

God's protection is a shield for those who have chosen to trust him as their Savior. No matter what happens, God's promise to watch over our souls and guard them for all eternity is our ultimate security and hope.

1 PETER 1:5 | Through your faith, God is protecting you by his power until you receive this salvation, which is ready to be revealed on the last day for all to see.

PSALM 18:30 | God's way is perfect. All the LORD's promises prove true. He is a shield for all who look to him for protection.

PSALM 121:2-3, 5, 8 | My help comes from the LORD, who made heaven and earth! He will not let you stumble; the one who watches over you will not slumber. . . . The LORD himself watches over you! The LORD stands beside you as your protective shade. . . . The LORD keeps watch over you as you come and go, both now and forever.

1 SAMUEL 2:9 | He will protect his faithful ones.

JOSHUA 23:10 | The LORD your God fights for you, just as he has promised.

PSALM 91:14 | The LORD says, "I will rescue those who love me. I will protect those who trust in my name."

The angel of the LORD is a guard; he surrounds and defends all who fear him.

PSALM 34:7

REDEMPTION

Redemption resonates deeply with the human heart. We love to see good things come out of bad situations. Perhaps we feel this way because we long for the broken pieces in our own lives to somehow be made whole. This is exactly what God promises to those who trust in his Son as their Savior and accept his sacrifice on the cross. They are forgiven, made clean and holy again, restored to right relationship with him, and guaranteed eternal life. No matter how messy, broken, or dirty your past is, God is able to use it for his good. If this truth is difficult for you to accept, reflect on God's promises of redemption in his Word. Trust that as time passes, you will see and experience him bringing beauty out of difficult situations in ways you would never have thought possible.

ISAIAH 44:22 | I have swept away your sins like a cloud. I have scattered your offenses like the morning mist. Oh, return to me, for I have paid the price to set you free.

PSALM 30:11 | You have turned my mourning into joyful dancing. You have taken away my clothes of mourning and clothed me with joy.

ROMANS 4:7-8 | Oh, what joy for those whose disobedience is forgiven, whose sins are put out of sight. Yes, what joy for those whose record the LORD has cleared of sin.

1 JOHN 1:8-9 | If we claim we have no sin, we are only fooling ourselves and not living in the truth. But if we confess our sins to him, he is faithful and just to forgive us our sins and to cleanse us from all wickedness.

ROMANS 8:28 | God causes everything to work together for the good of those who love God and are called according to his purpose for them.

Though your sins are like scarlet, I will make them as white as snow.

ISAIAH 1:18

REGRETS

If your regrets cause you to struggle with feelings of guilt, shame, and self-condemnation, then take some time to consider whether you've really accepted God's forgiveness for your sin. Your mind may believe so, but if your heart hasn't fully accepted this gift, then you aren't living in the freedom that God grants. God promises that if we faithfully confess our sins with a repentant heart and ask for his forgiveness, we are considered clean before him. Though this gift is free for our taking, it can sometimes be difficult to accept. God doesn't desire for you to punish yourself or live in shame from past mistakes. Receive his grace, hold your head high, and let go of your regrets, trusting his promise that he no longer thinks of the things you still regret.

ROMANS 3:23-24 | Everyone has sinned; we all fall short of God's glorious standard. Yet God, in his grace, freely makes us right in his sight. He did this through Christ Jesus when he freed us from the penalty for our sins.

2 CORINTHIANS 7:10 | The kind of sorrow God wants us to experience leads us away from sin and results in salvation. There's no regret for that kind of sorrow.

ISAIAH 43:25 | I—yes, I alone—will blot out your sins for my own sake and will never think of them again.

PROVERBS 28:13 | People who conceal their sins will not prosper, but if they confess and turn from them, they will receive mercy.

PSALM 32:5 | Finally, I confessed all my sins to you and stopped trying to hide my guilt. I said to myself, "I will confess my rebellion to the LORD."

And you forgave me! All my guilt is gone.

ACTS 10:43 | Everyone who believes in [Jesus] will have their sins forgiven through his name.

O Lord, you are so good, so ready to forgive, so full of unfailing love.

PSALM 86:5

REJECTION

Rejection has the power to make us feel unwanted, unloved, and even defective. Its sting can last a lifetime. Taking the high road after facing rejection is not an easy path, but it is one that leads to God's blessings. God promises that when you choose to bless others instead of retaliate, he will bless and reward you. When rejection has caused you to focus on your flaws and doubt all the good things about yourself, remember that God will never reject you. Come to him with your pain. Ask for his help to respond to rejection in a way that honors him, trusting that he will keep his promises to bless, defend, and comfort you.

2 CORINTHIANS 1:5 | The more we suffer for Christ, the more God will shower us with his comfort through Christ.

1 PETER 3:9 | Don't repay evil for evil. Don't retaliate with insults when people insult you. Instead, pay them back with a blessing. That is what God has called you to do, and he will grant you his blessing.

PROVERBS 25:21-22 | If your enemies are hungry, give them food to eat. If they are thirsty, give them water to drink. You will heap burning coals of shame on their heads, and the LORD will reward you.

LUKE 6:35 | Love your enemies! Do good to them. Lend to them without expecting to be repaid. Then your reward from heaven will be very great, and you will truly be acting as children of the Most High, for he is kind to those who are unthankful and wicked.

LUKE 6:22-23 | What blessings await you when people hate you and exclude you and mock you and curse you as evil because you follow the Son of Man. When that happens, be happy! Yes, leap for joy! For a great reward awaits you in heaven.

Every word of God proves true. He is a shield to all who come to him for protection.

PROVERBS 30:5

RESCUE

Is there something you desire to be rescued from? Maybe you long to be free from an impossible situation, a certain person, or even your own sin. Instead of trying to escape your circumstances, come to God, asking for him to rescue you and provide you with protection. The Bible promises that God helps us, saves us, defends us, and protects us in everything we face. God also promises that he will ultimately rescue those who believe in him from this evil world. The next time you wonder whether God can rescue you, remember that through his Son, he already has.

PSALM 121:1-2 | I look up to the mountains—
does my help come from there? My help comes
from the LORD, who made heaven and earth!

PSALM 40:17 | As for me, since I am poor and
needy, let the Lord keep me in his thoughts. You are
my helper and my savior. O my God, do not delay.

PSALM 12:5 | The LORD replies, "I have seen
violence done to the helpless, and I have heard the
groans of the poor. Now I will rise up to rescue
them, as they have longed for me to do."

PSALM 50:15 | Call on me when you are in trouble,
and I will rescue you, and you will give me glory.

EXODUS 14:13-14 | Don't be afraid. Just
stand still and watch the LORD rescue you.
. . . The LORD himself will fight for you.

GALATIANS 1:4 | Jesus gave his life for our sins,
just as God our Father planned, in order to rescue
us from this evil world in which we live.

PSALM 144:7 | Reach down from heaven
and rescue me; rescue me from deep waters,
from the power of my enemies.

We put our hope in the LORD. He is our help and our shield.

PSALM 33:20

RESENTMENT

When someone has wronged us, it feels easier to be angry than to be sad over the situation. However, when we allow our anger to linger too long within our hearts, it results in resentment. God doesn't promise we won't be betrayed, misunderstood, or unappreciated in this world. Every one of us will have our feelings hurt. But the key to keeping our hearts pure from resentment and bitterness is through the power of forgiveness. It is not easy to forgive someone who has caused us pain. But when we choose to resent that person instead of forgive him or her, the Bible tell us that our souls will be in danger. Is there resentment in your heart today? Who might God be calling you to forgive in order to experience freedom? Let go of your grudges and ask God to help you choose the path of forgiveness. If forgiveness feels impossible, reflect on Jesus' sacrifice on the cross and take to heart all the times your Father has forgiven you.

JAMES 5:9 | Don't grumble about each other, brothers and sisters, or you will be judged. For look—the Judge is standing at the door!

JOB 5:2 | Surely resentment destroys the fool, and jealousy kills the simple.

HEBREWS 12:15 | Look after each other so that none of you fails to receive the grace of God. Watch out that no poisonous root of bitterness grows up to trouble you, corrupting many.

JEREMIAH 3:22 | "My wayward children," says the LORD, "come back to me, and I will heal your wayward hearts."

LUKE 24:47 | There is forgiveness
of sins for all who repent.

ACTS 2:38 | Each of you must repent of your sins
and turn to God, and be baptized in the name of
Jesus Christ for the forgiveness of your sins.

*Forgive anyone you
are holding a grudge
against, so that your
Father in heaven will
forgive your sins, too.*

MARK 11:25

SACRIFICE

Have you ever felt tired of making sacrifices
for others? Have you felt like your own needs and
opportunities have been put on the back burner?
Even when we gladly make sacrifices for the people
we love, we sometimes need to be reminded that
they are worth it. God's Word promises many
benefits and blessings to living a sacrificial life.
Not only does God reward us; he says that he will
be pleased with us too. And pleasing God can
motivate us when we feel like we are continually
receiving the short end of the stick. The next time
you find yourself sacrificing your time, resources,

and energy for another, remember that God understands and empathizes with you. He made the ultimate sacrifice in giving up his own Son to take away your sins.

MARK 8:35 | If you try to hang on to your life, you will lose it. But if you give up your life for my sake and for the sake of the Good News, you will save it.

MATTHEW 10:42 | If you give even a cup of cold water to one of the least of my followers, you will surely be rewarded.

MATTHEW 19:29 | Everyone who has given up houses or brothers or sisters or father or mother or children or property, for my sake, will receive a hundred times as much in return and will inherit eternal life.

HEBREWS 9:27-28 | Just as each person is destined to die once and after that comes judgment, so also Christ was offered once for all time as a sacrifice to take away the sins of many people. He will come again, not to deal with our sins, but to bring salvation to all who are eagerly waiting for him.

GALATIANS 2:20 | My old self has been crucified with Christ. It is no longer I who live, but Christ lives in me. So I live in this earthly body by trusting in the Son of God, who loved me and gave himself for me.

Do good and . . . share with those in need. These are the sacrifices that please God.

HEBREWS 13:16

SALVATION

Many of us fall into the trap of thinking we need to work to earn our salvation. We give out of guilt. We serve to compensate for our sin. We go to church to feel like "good" people. We do all of this because it's easier to trust in our own efforts than to trust in God's promises. His promise of salvation is simple: If we trust that Jesus is Lord, sent to earth by God to take away our sins, then we will be saved. That's it. This means you don't need to try so hard; the work has already been done. Don't allow Satan to complicate God's beautiful gift of grace. Remind yourself today of God's promises of salvation, and find peace in the fact that your belief in Jesus has made you right with God.

ROMANS 10:9-10 | If you openly declare that Jesus is Lord and believe in your heart that God raised him from the dead, you will be saved. For it is by believing in your heart that you are made right with God, and it is by openly declaring your faith that you are saved.

EZEKIEL 18:21 | If wicked people turn away from all their sins and begin to obey my decrees and do what is just and right, they will surely live and not die.

JOHN 5:24 | I tell you the truth, those who listen to my message and believe in God who sent me have eternal life. They will never be condemned for their sins, but they have already passed from death into life.

JOHN 3:16 | This is how God loved the world: He gave his one and only Son, so that everyone who believes in him will not perish but have eternal life.

EPHESIANS 1:11 | Because we are united with Christ, we have received an inheritance from God, for he chose us in advance, and he makes everything work out according to his plan.

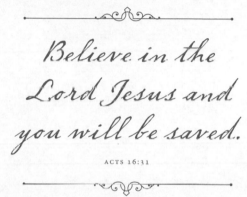

Believe in the Lord Jesus and you will be saved.

ACTS 16:31

SATISFACTION

Have you ever felt disappointed in a person
or thing because it failed to satisfy your expectations
or needs? The reality is that God has placed a longing for heaven inside of every human heart. Nothing
on this earth can bring true fulfillment and lasting
happiness—they come only through him. The Bible
promises over and over that God is able to satisfy—
to meet that deep emptiness inside us that longs to
be full. It is only a relationship with him that can
truly lead to a life that is rich and satisfying. Do you
believe you can be content in God alone? The next
time you find yourself longing for more in life, come

to God with your disappointments. Remember his promises to satisfy those who believe in him and continually seek his face.

PSALM 107:8-9 | Let them praise the LORD for his great love and for the wonderful things he has done for them. For he satisfies the thirsty and fills the hungry with good things.

JOHN 6:35 | Jesus replied, "I am the bread of life. Whoever comes to me will never be hungry again. Whoever believes in me will never be thirsty."

PSALM 63:1, 5 | O God, you are my God.... My soul thirsts for you.... You satisfy me more than the richest feast.

PSALM 17:15 | When I awake, I will see you face to face and be satisfied.

JOHN 4:13-14 | Jesus replied, "Anyone who drinks this water will soon become thirsty again. But those who drink the water I give will never be thirsty again. It becomes a fresh, bubbling spring within them, giving them eternal life."

HEBREWS 13:5 | Don't love money; be satisfied with what you have. For God has said, "I will never fail you. I will never abandon you."

1 TIMOTHY 6:6-8 | True godliness with contentment is itself great wealth. After all, we brought nothing with us when we came into the world, and we can't take anything with us when we leave it. So if we have enough food and clothing, let us be content.

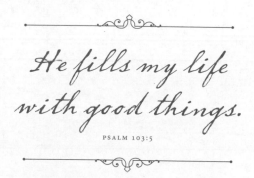

He fills my life with good things.

PSALM 103:5

SECURITY

The heart of every woman longs for security. From the troubles we face in our finances, marriages, and homes to the concerns we have about our work and world, we all have moments when we wish someone would promise us that everything will be okay. The truth is, God has already promised us who are believers in Christ that we will be kept safe for all eternity because of our faith. He has assured us, too, of a priceless inheritance stored up for us in heaven. Even though we live in a hostile and unpredictable world, we can feel secure in how the story will end. Allow your heart to be at rest, trusting that God is your refuge and nothing can snatch you from his hand.

1 PETER 1:4 | We have a priceless inheritance—an inheritance that is kept in heaven for you, pure and undefiled, beyond the reach of change and decay.

1 CORINTHIANS 2:9 | No eye has seen, no ear has heard, and no mind has imagined what God has prepared for those who love him.

ROMANS 5:1-2 | Therefore, since we have been made right in God's sight by faith, we have peace with God because of what Jesus Christ our Lord has done for us. Because of our faith, Christ has brought us into this place of undeserved privilege where we now stand, and we confidently and joyfully look forward to sharing God's glory.

JOHN 10:28-29 | I give them eternal life, and they will never perish. No one can snatch them away from me, for my Father has given them to me, and he is more powerful than anyone else. No one can snatch them from the Father's hand.

PROVERBS 14:26 | Those who fear the LORD are secure; he will be a refuge for their children.

PSALM 75:3 | When the earth quakes and its people live in turmoil, I am the one who keeps its foundations firm.

The LORD is your security. He will keep your foot from being caught in a trap.

PROVERBS 3:26

SELF-ESTEEM

As women, our sense of self is often attacked because of what the world says we should look like or become. Our self-esteem shatters when we see ourselves differently than how God sees us. Rather than telling yourself who you *should be*, rest in who your Creator says *you are*. The words he uses to describe you are "loved," "valuable," "precious," "a masterpiece," and "his child." How might you carry yourself if you truly believed that this is how God sees you? Ask God to take away the lies that tempt you to doubt your worth. The best way to do this is to read

God's promises, remembering that the almighty God speaks these things over *you* personally.

MATTHEW 10:29-31 | Not a single sparrow can fall to the ground without your Father knowing it. And the very hairs on your head are all numbered. So don't be afraid; you are more valuable to God than a whole flock of sparrows.

PSALM 8:5 | You made [human beings] only a little lower than God and crowned them with glory and honor.

GALATIANS 3:26 | You are all children of God through faith in Christ Jesus.

EPHESIANS 1:4-6 | Even before he made the world, God loved us and chose us in Christ to be holy and without fault in his eyes. God decided in advance to adopt us into his own family by bringing us to himself through Jesus Christ. This is what he wanted to do, and it gave him great pleasure. So we praise

God for the glorious grace he has poured
out on us who belong to his dear Son.

EPHESIANS 2:10 | We are God's masterpiece. He
has created us anew in Christ Jesus, so we can do
the good things he planned for us long ago.

*How precious are
your thoughts
about me, O God.
They cannot be
numbered!*

PSALM 139:17

SHAME

The message of guilt is I've done something bad. The message of shame is *I am bad.* Have you experienced the difference? Shame is not something God uses for our spiritual growth. In fact, shame is not from God at all. When the evil one tries to convince you that you are unlovable, unworthy, and beyond help, listen to God's voice telling you how much you are loved, known, and redeemed. His voice can clearly be heard through his promises in his Word. What you have done in the past or where you have been does not define you. You can be a woman who walks with confidence because God promises he won't condemn anyone who belongs to him.

PSALM 3:3 | You, O LORD, are a shield around me;
you are my glory, the one who holds my head high.

ISAIAH 54:4 | Fear not; you will no
longer live in shame. Don't be afraid;
there is no more disgrace for you.

PSALM 51:1-3, 17 | Have mercy on me, O
God, because of your unfailing love. Because
of your great compassion, blot out the stain of
my sins. Wash me clean from my guilt. Purify
me from my sin. For I recognize my rebellion;
it haunts me day and night. . . . The sacrifice
you desire is a broken spirit. You will not
reject a broken and repentant heart, O God.

ROMANS 3:22 | We are made right with God by
placing our faith in Jesus Christ. And this is true
for everyone who believes, no matter who we are.

MICAH 7:19 | Once again you will have compassion on us. You will trample our sins under your feet and throw them into the depths of the ocean!

There is no condemnation for those who belong to Christ Jesus.

ROMANS 8:1

SPIRITUAL GROWTH

Spiritual growth is not just something to gain on this earth; it becomes a part of you for all eternity. With this in mind, do not be discouraged when you feel you're at a spiritual standstill or aren't growing enough in your walk. Remember that God promises to nourish you and produce fruit in your life, correct and teach you, and continue his work in you until it is finished. He is the master gardener who carefully watches over and tends your spiritual growth. Your job is to continually seek him in his Word and prayerfully invite him into every moment of your life. Guard your heart and invest your

time in the only thing that will last forever—your
relationship with your Savior.

ISAIAH 58:11 | The LORD will guide you
continually, giving you water when you are dry
and restoring your strength. You will be like a
well-watered garden, like an ever-flowing spring.

ISAIAH 55:10-11 | The rain and snow come
down from the heavens and stay on the ground
to water the earth. They cause the grain to grow,
producing seed for the farmer and bread for the
hungry. It is the same with my word. I send it out,
and it always produces fruit. It will accomplish all I
want it to, and it will prosper everywhere I send it.

2 TIMOTHY 3:16-17 | All Scripture is inspired
by God and is useful to teach us what is true and
to make us realize what is wrong in our lives.
It corrects us when we are wrong and teaches
us to do what is right. God uses it to prepare
and equip his people to do every good work.

1 TIMOTHY 4:8 | Physical training is good, but training for godliness is much better, promising benefits in this life and in the life to come.

God, who began the good work within you, will continue his work.

PHILIPPIANS 1:6

STARTING OVER

Have you ever dreamed of a new beginning—an escape from the ordinary or a chance to wipe the slate clean and start fresh? No matter what mistakes plague your past or what sins are a present struggle, it is never too late to start over. In fact, God's Word promises that those who ask Jesus to be their Savior and believe in him become new people; their old life is gone and a new one has begun. God will continually do new things within the hearts of believers if they allow him to. God is doing something new within your heart today. Do you see it? Rejoice in the fact that you have a God who delights in fresh starts, second chances, and new beginnings.

2 CORINTHIANS 5:17 | Anyone who belongs
to Christ has become a new person. The
old life is gone; a new life has begun!

REVELATION 21:5 | The one sitting on the throne
said, "Look, I am making everything new!"

ZECHARIAH 4:10 | Do not despise these small
beginnings, for the LORD rejoices to see the work begin.

ISAIAH 43:19 | I am about to do something
new. See, I have already begun! Do you not see
it? I will make a pathway through the wilderness.
I will create rivers in the dry wasteland.

TITUS 3:5 | He washed away our sins, giving us a
new birth and new life through the Holy Spirit.

LUKE 6:21 | God blesses you who are hungry
now, for you will be satisfied. God blesses you
who weep now, for in due time you will laugh.

STRESS

Have you ever felt incapable of managing the daily pressures of life? You are not alone. Women today juggle their marriages, family schedules, and careers with responsibilities in their households, friendships, and ministries. But you were not made to handle all of this on your own. God doesn't place high expectations on your schedule. He simply desires for you to come to him when life becomes too much. If you are in a season of stress, set your calendar aside and spend some time with God. He is waiting for you to call on him. He promises to carry your heavy burdens so you can experience peace and rest for your soul.

PSALM 119:143 | As pressure and stress bear down on me, I find joy in your commands.

PSALM 86:7 | I will call to you whenever I'm in trouble, and you will answer me.

2 CORINTHIANS 4:8-9 | We are pressed on every side by troubles, but we are not crushed. We are perplexed, but not driven to despair. We are hunted down, but never abandoned by God.

MATTHEW 11:28-29 | Jesus said, "Come to me, all of you who are weary and carry heavy burdens, and I will give you rest. Take my yoke upon you. Let me teach you, because I am humble and gentle at heart, and you will find rest for your souls."

TEMPTATION

Are you aware of which sins tempt you most? Do you know when you are vulnerable to Satan's attacks? Have you considered the impact your thoughts have on your heart? If your heart determines the course of your life, then guarding it is one of the most important things you can do. But you cannot do this without God's help. God promises that when you remain close to him, he will help you have self-control, guide your thoughts, and show you a way out of temptation. When opportunities arise and you have to make a choice, remember God's promises. He is always ready to help in times of temptation.

GALATIANS 5:22-23 | The Holy Spirit produces
this kind of fruit in our lives: . . . self-control.

1 CORINTHIANS 10:13 | The temptations in your
life are no different from what others experience. And
God is faithful. He will not allow the temptation to be
more than you can stand. When you are tempted, he
will show you a way out so that you can endure.

2 PETER 1:5-6 | Supplement your . . . knowledge
with self-control, and self-control with patient
endurance, and patient endurance with godliness.

PSALM 119:9 | How can a young person
stay pure? By obeying your word.

ROMANS 8:6 | Letting your sinful nature control
your mind leads to death. But letting the Spirit
control your mind leads to life and peace.

PROVERBS 4:23 | Guard your heart above all
else, for it determines the course of your life.

THANKFULNESS

We live in a world filled with less-than-perfect days and unpredictable circumstances. We experience ups and downs and never know what's around the corner. However, choosing to be thankful has the power to lift us above our circumstances, change our perspectives, and shape the way we see God and the world. Thankfulness keeps us connected to God no matter what life has in store. If it is difficult for you to find things to be thankful for, meditate on God's promises. Allow them to transform your heart so you may see all of life as a gift to enjoy instead of a burden to bear.

COLOSSIANS 2:6-7 | Just as you accepted Christ Jesus as your Lord, you must continue to follow him. Let your roots grow down into him, and let your lives be built on him. Then your faith will grow strong in the truth you were taught, and you will overflow with thankfulness.

1 CHRONICLES 16:34 | Give thanks to the LORD, for he is good! His faithful love endures forever.

1 CORINTHIANS 15:57 | Thank God! He gives us victory over sin and death through our Lord Jesus Christ.

PSALM 50:23 | Giving thanks is a sacrifice that truly honors me. If you keep to my path, I will reveal to you the salvation of God.

PSALM 147:1 | Praise the LORD! How good to sing praises to our God! How delightful and how fitting!

1 THESSALONIANS 5:18 | Be thankful in all circumstances, for this is God's will for you who belong to Christ Jesus.

TRANSITIONS

Along with every stage of life come transitions. And these changes, whether good or bad, can feel disorienting and scary. When life throws a curveball your way, hang on to God's promises. God never changes, which means you can always count on him. God also promises to be with you no matter what transitions loom ahead. Whether you are changing churches, jobs, or locations, God is already there, waiting for you. He promises to be your faithful guide and constant companion wherever you go.

HEBREWS 13:8 | Jesus Christ is the same
yesterday, today, and forever.

MARK 13:31 | Heaven and earth will disappear,
but my words will never disappear.

JAMES 1:17 | Whatever is good and perfect is
a gift coming down to us from God our Father,
who created all the lights in the heavens. He
never changes or casts a shifting shadow.

JOSHUA 1:9 | Be strong and courageous! Do
not be afraid or discouraged. For the LORD
your God is with you wherever you go.

MALACHI 3:6 | I am the LORD, and I do not change.

ISAIAH 40:8 | The grass withers and the flowers
fade, but the word of our God stands forever.

ISAIAH 41:13 | I hold you by your right
hand—I, the LORD your God. And I say to you,
"Don't be afraid. I am here to help you."

EXODUS 3:12 | God answered, "I will be with you."

TRIALS

Trials have a way of flipping our faith upside down. They force us to confront our deep beliefs about God and raise questions like, *Is God really good? Does he hear my prayers? Will he help me find a way out of this?* How can we allow the trials in our lives to strengthen our faith instead of destroying it? The best way is to meditate on God's promises in his Word. Doing so reminds us of who God is and keeps us aware of his presence. You may not understand why God has called you to walk through a particular crisis, but he

promises to be right beside you through it, to grow
you, and to work all of it into something good.
Remember that you will have to endure these trials
for only a little while. An eternity of wonderful joy
lies ahead.

2 CHRONICLES 15:4 | Whenever they were
in trouble and turned to the LORD, the God of
Israel, and sought him out, they found him.

1 PETER 1:7 | These trials will show that your
faith is genuine. It is being tested as fire tests
and purifies gold—though your faith is far more
precious than mere gold. So when your faith
remains strong through many trials, it will bring
you much praise and glory and honor on the day
when Jesus Christ is revealed to the whole world.

ISAIAH 43:2 | When you go through deep waters,
I will be with you. When you go through rivers
of difficulty, you will not drown. When you walk
through the fire of oppression, you will not be
burned up; the flames will not consume you.

PSALM 126:5-6 | Those who plant in tears will harvest with shouts of joy. They weep as they go to plant their seed, but they sing as they return with the harvest.

ROMANS 8:28 | God causes everything to work together for the good of those who love God and are called according to his purpose for them.

There is wonderful joy ahead, even though you must endure many trials for a little while.

1 PETER 1:6

TRUSTING GOD

Do you dwell on problems, give in to worry, or try to control the future? Jesus tells his followers not to be anxious, yet so many believers spend their lives fretting over circumstances they cannot control. Trusting God means believing he is loving and good and that he wants (and is able!) to bless your life. Trusting God is not only a moment-by-moment decision, but also a lifelong discipline. Come to God as a little child, simply telling him your worries and fears. Watch how he transforms your life as you read his Word and choose to believe his promises that he is worthy of your trust.

271

NAHUM 1:7 | The Lord is good, a strong refuge when trouble comes. He is close to those who trust in him.

PSALM 125:1 | Those who trust in the Lord are as secure as Mount Zion; they will not be defeated but will endure forever.

PROVERBS 3:5-6 | Trust in the Lord with all your heart; do not depend on your own understanding. Seek his will in all you do, and he will show you which path to take.

PSALM 84:12 | O Lord of Heaven's Armies, what joy for those who trust in you.

JEREMIAH 17:7-8 | Blessed are those who trust in the Lord and have made the Lord their hope and confidence. They are like trees planted along a riverbank, with roots that reach deep into the water. Such trees are not bothered by the heat or worried by long months of drought. Their leaves stay green, and they never stop producing fruit.

PSALM 37:5 | Commit everything you do to the LORD. Trust him, and he will help you.

HEBREWS 10:23 | Let us hold tightly without wavering to the hope we affirm, for God can be trusted to keep his promise.

———————

Trust in the LORD always, for the LORD GOD is the eternal Rock.

ISAIAH 26:4

———————

VICTORY

In a world with so much sadness, it can be tempting to believe that Satan has already gained the victory. But the story is not over yet. God promises that no matter what trials or sorrows we face during our time on earth, he has already overcome the world. This means that by his power, he gives us victory over sin, evil, and even death. Read his promises of victory, and remember that the God you serve is a mighty warrior who will never stop fighting for those he loves.

REVELATION 11:15 | The world has now become the Kingdom of our Lord and of his Christ, and he will reign forever and ever.

JOHN 16:33 | Here on earth you will have many trials and sorrows. But take heart, because I have overcome the world.

1 JOHN 5:4 | Every child of God defeats this evil world, and we achieve this victory through our faith.

1 CORINTHIANS 15:57 | Thank God! He gives us victory over sin and death through our Lord Jesus Christ.

PSALM 98:2 | The LORD has announced his victory and has revealed his righteousness to every nation!

EXODUS 15:3 | The LORD is a warrior; Yahweh is his name!

JUDGES 4:14 | Get ready! This is the day the LORD will give you victory . . . for the LORD is marching ahead of you.

ISAIAH 42:13 | The LORD will march forth like a mighty hero; he will come out like a warrior, full of fury. He will shout his battle cry and crush all his enemies.

Overwhelming victory is ours through Christ, who loved us.

ROMANS 8:37

WAITING

We're not always good at waiting. It requires being still and passive, allowing God to unfold matters in his timing when we desire quick fixes to our problems. But sometimes God doesn't answer our prayers right away because real spiritual growth develops in the waiting and the watching. We are continually confronted with the choice to either despair or trust. The Bible promises that those who choose to trust during times of waiting will be blessed with strength, hope, and confidence. What prayer are you still waiting for God to answer? Read his promises to you in his Word, and be encouraged that he is doing great things in your heart as you patiently wait for him to act.

MICAH 7:7 | As for me, I look to the LORD for help. I wait confidently for God to save me, and my God will certainly hear me.

PSALM 62:1, 5 | I wait quietly before God, for my victory comes from him.... Let all that I am wait quietly before God, for my hope is in him.

PSALM 59:9 | You are my strength; I wait for you to rescue me, for you, O God, are my fortress.

ISAIAH 33:2 | LORD, be merciful to us, for we have waited for you. Be our strong arm each day and our salvation in times of trouble.

ISAIAH 30:18 | The LORD must wait for you to come to him so he can show you his love and compassion. For the LORD is a faithful God. Blessed are those who wait for his help.

WEARINESS

As a woman, do you sometimes place expectations on yourself to do everything and be everything for the people in your life? It can be hard to accept your limitations. But this kind of pressure will inevitably leave you feeling weary. When you finally hit your breaking point or decide you just can't do it all anymore, there is only one place to turn. Go to God in your weariness. He promises to respond graciously. In fact, he assures us that being in his presence will not only give us rest, but it will also give us strength! Take a break from your routine and find peace in the presence of the Lord today. Accept his invitation to restore your mind, body, and heart.

PSALM 127:1-2 | Unless the LORD builds a house, the work of the builders is wasted. Unless the LORD protects a city, guarding it with sentries will do no good. It is useless for you to work so hard from early morning until late at night, anxiously working for food to eat; for God gives rest to his loved ones.

ISAIAH 40:29-31 | He gives power to the weak and strength to the powerless. Even youths will become weak and tired, and young men will fall in exhaustion. But those who trust in the LORD will find new strength. They will soar high on wings like eagles. They will run and not grow weary. They will walk and not faint.

PSALM 91:1 | Those who live in the shelter of the Most High will find rest in the shadow of the Almighty.

PSALM 23:2-3 | He lets me rest in green meadows; he leads me beside peaceful streams. He renews my strength.

PSALM 28:7 | The LORD is my strength
and shield. I trust him with all my heart.
He helps me, and my heart is filled with joy.
I burst out in songs of thanksgiving.

PSALM 68:35 | God is awesome in
his sanctuary. The God of Israel gives
power and strength to his people.

There is a special rest still waiting for the people of God.

HEBREWS 4:9

WISDOM

Every woman has certain areas in her life that require delicate care—maybe a situation at work or a difficult relationship or the struggle to raise godly children. How can she handle these challenges wisely? God promises that those who seek wisdom will live a life that is successful, solid, and honoring to him. He also promises he is faithful to give wisdom to those who ask. When you go to God with your request, ask yourself these questions: *Am I in his Word? Do I take time to listen to him when I pray? Am I actively fighting against sin in my life?* If you can answer yes to these questions, you are on the path to wisdom. Spend time with God, reflect on these promises, and allow him to teach you his ways.

PROVERBS 3:13 | Joyful is the person who finds wisdom, the one who gains understanding.

PROVERBS 4:11-12 | I will teach you wisdom's ways and lead you in straight paths. When you walk, you won't be held back; when you run, you won't stumble.

PROVERBS 9:11 | Wisdom will multiply your days and add years to your life.

JAMES 1:5 | If you need wisdom, ask our generous God, and he will give it to you. He will not rebuke you for asking.

MATTHEW 7:24 | Anyone who listens to my teaching and follows it is wise, like a person who builds a house on solid rock.

PSALM 111:10 | Fear of the LORD is the
foundation of true wisdom. All who obey his
commandments will grow in wisdom.

ECCLESIASTES 2:26 | God gives wisdom,
knowledge, and joy to those who please him.

PROVERBS 1:23 | Come and listen to my counsel.
I'll share my heart with you and make you wise.

HOSEA 14:9 | Let those who are wise understand
these things. Let those with discernment listen
carefully. The paths of the LORD are true and right,
and righteous people live by walking in them.
But in those paths sinners stumble and fall.

PSALM 119:24 | Your laws please me;
they give me wise advice.

WITNESSING

To witness simply means to tell others about something you have experienced. The story of how you met Jesus and grew to love him is the greatest story you could ever tell. For many of us, it's scary to openly discuss our faith with others. But when we do, God promises to be with us, giving us his strength and power. How might the Lord be encouraging you to witness to your friends, coworkers, children, or even your spouse? Ask the Lord to help you become familiar with your own story, recognizing his loving presence in your life and the blessings he has bestowed, and then pray for courage to tell it. When you publicly acknowledge the Lord here on earth, he will acknowledge you in the presence of his angels.

2 TIMOTHY 1:7-8 | God has not given us a spirit of fear and timidity, but of power, love, and self-discipline. So never be ashamed to tell others about our Lord.... With the strength God gives you, be ready to suffer with me for the sake of the Good News.

1 PETER 2:12 | Be careful to live properly among your unbelieving neighbors. Then even if they accuse you of doing wrong, they will see your honorable behavior, and they will give honor to God when he judges the world.

LUKE 12:8 | Everyone who acknowledges me publicly here on earth, the Son of Man will also acknowledge in the presence of God's angels.

ACTS 18:9-10 | One night the Lord spoke to Paul in a vision and told him, "Don't be afraid! Speak out! Don't be silent! For I am with you."

WORD OF GOD

The Bible isn't just a book written
by godly people thousands of years ago; it is the
recorded voice of God and one of the main ways he
communicates with us. How amazing that the God
of the universe actually wants to communicate with
us! The Bible has the power to shape our hearts,
minds, and souls, and it provides us with joy and
purpose in life. It helps us avoid sin and its disas-
trous consequences, among many other benefits.
No matter what season of life you are in, God has
something to say to you through his Word. Open
up your Bible and experience the many blessings

promised to those who allow God's Word to guide
their lives.

PSALM 119:105 | Your word is a lamp to
guide my feet and a light for my path.

HEBREWS 4:12 | The word of God is alive and powerful.
It is sharper than the sharpest two-edged sword, cutting
between soul and spirit, between joint and marrow.
It exposes our innermost thoughts and desires.

ISAIAH 40:8 | The grass withers and the flowers
fade, but the word of our God stands forever.

JEREMIAH 15:16 | When I discovered
your words, I devoured them. They are
my joy and my heart's delight.

JOHN 8:32 | You will know the truth,
and the truth will set you free.

JOHN 12:50 | I know his commands
lead to eternal life.

PROVERBS 6:23 | Their command is a
lamp and their instruction a light.

HEBREWS 8:10 | I will put my laws in their
minds, and I will write them on their hearts.

* * *

Blessed are all who
hear the word of
God and put it
into practice.

LUKE 11:28

* * *

WORK

God's plan for our lives is to work, and our efforts matter to him. However, we all go through seasons when our work feels dull, frustrating, and meaningless. Whether you work in the corporate world or at home, it has value to God. He searches for those who work with perseverance, courage, and enthusiasm. If you feel unfulfilled by your job, ask God to change your attitude as you reflect on his promises. Walk into work each day looking for opportunities to serve God and others. God promises that when you have this perspective, he will reward you. Take heart in the truth that nothing you do for the Lord is ever meaningless.

1 CORINTHIANS 15:58 | My dear brothers and sisters, be strong and immovable. Always work enthusiastically for the Lord, for you know that nothing you do for the Lord is ever useless.

DEUTERONOMY 28:12 | The LORD will send rain at the proper time from his rich treasury in the heavens and will bless all the work you do.

COLOSSIANS 3:23-24 | Work willingly at whatever you do, as though you were working for the Lord rather than for people. Remember that the Lord will give you an inheritance as your reward, and that the Master you are serving is Christ.

HEBREWS 6:10 | God is not unjust. He will not forget how hard you have worked for him and how you have shown your love to him by caring for other believers, as you still do.

2 CHRONICLES 15:7 | As for you, be strong and courageous, for your work will be rewarded.

Commit your actions to the LORD, and your plans will succeed.

PROVERBS 16:3

WORRY

Worrying doesn't make a problem go away or prepare us for it. The only thing worrying does is consume us—our time, energy, faith, and trust in God. What worries weigh on your heart today? If Jesus were right beside you, what do you think he would say? When you look to God's Word, you can be assured that Jesus will care for you, lead you, and give you everything you need. Tell him what burdens you face today and then release them into his control. Remember that if he cares so wonderfully for something as small as a flower, he surely cares for you.

MATTHEW 6:31-33 | Don't worry about these things, saying, "What will we eat? What will we drink? What will we wear?" These things dominate the thoughts of unbelievers, but your heavenly Father already knows all your needs. Seek the Kingdom of God above all else, and live righteously, and he will give you everything you need.

ISAIAH 40:11 | He will feed his flock like a shepherd. He will carry the lambs in his arms, holding them close to his heart. He will gently lead the mother sheep with their young.

MATTHEW 6:30 | If God cares so wonderfully for wildflowers that are here today and thrown into the fire tomorrow, he will certainly care for you. Why do you have so little faith?

WORSHIP

Human beings were created to worship, and true worship begins when we praise God for who he is and all he has done. Throughout God's Word, we see his people reflecting on his promises and praising him in response. Perhaps your soul is in need of worship. Think about what God has done in your life recently and rejoice in his presence. Allow these promises from Scripture to encourage you to praise God—and experience a foretaste of the joy and celebration you will one day experience in heaven.

PSALM 13:5-6 | I trust in your unfailing love. I will rejoice because you have rescued me. I will sing to the LORD because he is good to me.

2 THESSALONIANS 1:10 | When he comes on that day, he will receive glory from his holy people—praise from all who believe. And this includes you, for you believed what we told you about him.

ISAIAH 25:1 | O LORD, I will honor and praise your name, for you are my God. You do such wonderful things! You planned them long ago, and now you have accomplished them.

PSALM 59:17 | O my Strength, to you I sing praises, for you, O God, are my refuge, the God who shows me unfailing love.

REVELATION 4:11 | You are worthy, O Lord our God, to receive glory and honor and power. For you created all things, and they exist because you created what you pleased.

PSALM 95:6-7 | Come, let us worship and bow down. Let us kneel before the LORD our maker, for he is our God. We are the people he watches over, the flock under his care.

HEBREWS 12:28-29 | Since we are receiving a Kingdom that is unshakable, let us be thankful and please God by worshiping him with holy fear and awe. For our God is a devouring fire.

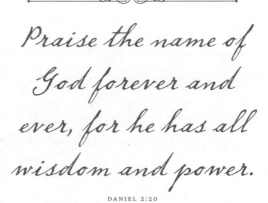

Praise the name of God forever and ever, for he has all wisdom and power.

DANIEL 2:20